James A. Berlin and Social-Epistemic Rhetorics
A Seminar

James A. Berlin

JAMES A. BERLIN AND SOCIAL-EPISTEMIC RHETORICS

A Seminar

Victor J. Vitanza

Parlor Press
Anderson, South Carolina
www.parlorpress.com

Parlor Press LLC, Anderson, South Carolina, 29621

© 2021 by Parlor Press
All rights reserved.
Printed in the United States of America
S A N: 2 5 4 - 8 8 7 9

Library of Congress Cataloging-in-Publication Data

Names: Vitanza, Victor J., author.
Title: James A. Berlin and social-epistemic rhetorics : a seminar / Victor J. Vitanza.
Description: Anderson, South Carolina : Parlor Press, 2021. | Includes bibliographical references. | Summary: "Rhetoric and composition have, at last, received a long-lost message in the form of Victor J. Vitanza's seminar at the University of Texas at Austin, on James A. Berlin, who developed methods to critique the socially constructed, politically charged reality of classrooms and culture"-- Provided by publisher.
Identifiers: LCCN 2021026611 (print) | LCCN 2021026612 (ebook) | ISBN 9781643172200 (paperback) | ISBN 9781643172217 (pdf) | ISBN 9781643172224 (epub)
Subjects: LCSH: English language--Rhetoric--Study and teaching--United States. | Academic writing--Study and teaching--United States. | English language--Rhetoric--Study and teaching--Authorship. | Composition
(Language arts)--Study and teaching. | Rhetoric--Study and teaching--Research--Methodology. | Berlin, James A.--Influence. | LCGFT: Lectures.
Classification: LCC PE1405.U6 V48 2021 (print) | LCC PE1405.U6 (ebook) | DDC 808--dc23
LC record available at https://lccn.loc.gov/2021026611
LC ebook record available at https://lccn.loc.gov/2021026612

978-1-64317-220-0 (paperback)
978-1-64317-221-7 (pdf)
978-1-64317-222-4 (epub)

2 3 4 5

Book design by David Blakesley.
Printed on acid-free paper.

Parlor Press, LLC is an independent publisher of scholarly and trade titles in print and multimedia formats. This book is available in paperback and ebook formats from Parlor Press on the World Wide Web at http://www.parlorpress.com or through online and brick-and-mortar bookstores. For submission information or to find out about Parlor Press publications, write to Parlor Press, 3015 Brackenberry Drive, Anderson, South Carolina, 29621, or email editor@parlorpress.com.

Contents

Foreword *ix*

Introduction *13*

Week #1 *19*

Week #2 *24*

Week #3 *33*

Week #4 *46*

Week #5 *51*

Week #6 *55*

Week #7 *65*

Week #8 *71*

Week #9 *81*

Week #10 *91*

Week #11 *102*

Weeks #12-13 *112*

Weeks #14-15 *113*

Appendices *116*

For Jim and our students

Foreword

The "IT" of It All

When "IT" happened, I was teaching, conducting a seminar on rhetoric with a large group of humanities students. One of the students had brought copies of the *NYTimes Magazine* article on Jacques Derrida. We spent the opening moments of the seminar reading aloud from it. There's a particular passage that sticks, will ever stick, in my mind. The article, if it has a topoi, is "the experience of the impossible," That is, the experience of death. In the article Derrida thinks outlaid about death, his death. He says: "It is true that I'm obsessed with death. I am at every minute attentive to the possibility that in the following hour I will be dead and the person I am with will say, 'I was just in the room with I'm, and he is dead.'"

About fifteen minutes later, my wife, Toni, knocked on the door of the seminar room where I was ruminating on the topos life is a "tissue of contingencies" (I was thinking out loud about Richard Rorty's phrase in contingency, irony, and solidarity). I opened that door and Toni called me outside to the hall. She told me that Janice Lauer had requested that she find me immediately to let me know what? That JB had died of a heart attack.

I lost "it." Now, I must find it again. But how and where? Opening. . . . You step out of a room. . . . A message is delivered. . . . You return to the room, and yet you don't. And you say, I said, to my class, that I could not continue. I explained that I was just in my life with a friend, and now he is dead.

It will have taken me a long, long time to wrestle with this angel, left, far left unsaid. After all, you and I both know, all too well, that impossibility will by necessity remain, even if said, will remain undelivered. In a sense—but I hope not in all senses, undelivered. I would prefer not to not think that what remains unsaid stays undelivered.

In these situations that we find ourselves thrown into, by chance? We (should I simply say "I") need to try to get our (my) bearings. Both public and private.

Public and private: In a piece of epideictic discourse that Jim had most recently written about the journal and me, he says: "PRE/TEXT is a forum where we can all get together to disagree, establishing relationships, as V.V. and I have done, on mutual and heartfelt disrespect. (I could never be troubled to argue with a position or person I did not genuinely dislike at least part of the time. It is out of scorn that worthwhile differences are discovered. Without rancor there is no rose.)"

–/\/\/\ *Published in PRE/TEXT Vol. 14 1-2*

Introduction

Seminar on James A. Berlin, Rhetoric as Social-Epistemic, Offered Fall 1998 and Again Fall 2001 at University of Texas at Arlington

The two Seminars I am recalling will focus on what is called social-epistemic rhetoric as it was developed primarily by James A. Berlin. (Simply defined, a social-epistemic rhetoric is one that has as its epistemology a view that reality is socially-constructed and that has as its politics a radical socialist set of agendas.)

We will read Berlin's three books and numerous articles as well as work done by others in support of (Patricia Bizzell, John Trimbur, etc.) and in critical response to this rhetoric (Linda Flower, Peter Elbow, etc.). To study the works of Berlin is to study the field of composition from the mid-eighties to the present day.

Berlin's Topologies thoroughly and perpetually re-mapped the field and, therefore, determined what could be said and not said about composition theories and pedagogies; what could be thought about textbooks in the field and what could not be thought; what could be seen as ethically and politically acceptable reasons for teaching literacy and what could not.

About the plotting of the syllabus: I have arranged our study of James A. Berlin from four incremental perspectives: His constantly revised Theories and Topologies of Composition Studies, Histories/historiographies of Rhetoric and Composition; and his views on Composition Studies, Ideology, and Cultural Studies (The Social-Epistemic Paths); and his Final, Posthumous Statements.

I begin the syllabus by way of the historical context of the NEH seminar, in which JB was introduced to rhetoric/composition. (I was not only an observer but also a participant myself in this seminar.) Moreover, in the plotting of the weekly syllabus, I have referred to what I call two major articles.

Please understand that these articles are in my judgment "major." Other people would, of course, plot and unfold the syllabus differently, with perhaps other articles, focuses, and emphases.

Seminar participants will be expected to write 10 one-page, single-spaced position papers specifically based on the readings; and will be expected to write one thoroughly researched paper for publication. (The topic must be approved by the instructor.) The one-page papers are to exhibit a careful understanding of JB's arguments and an interrogation of them. These will be published on the Hyper News site and then responded to by seminar participants and any other public subscriber to the seminar and the list.

* Students and interested people could subscribe to Berlin-L — Helen Foster, Michelle Ballif, Ron Hugar, Diane Davis, Matthew Levy, Collin Brooke Janice Lauer, Cynthia Haynes, Michelle Sidler, Paul Kei Matsuda, Robert Inkster, David Rieder, Alan Taylor, Tom Rickert, Jenny Bay, Kara Robinson, Byron Hawk, Victor J. Vitanza.

Texts

Berlin, James A. *Rhetorics, Poetics, and Cultures: Refiguring College English Studies*. Paper. NCTE.
—. *Rhetoric and Reality: Writing Instruction in American Colleges, 1900–1985*. Paper. NCTE.
—. *Writing Instruction in Nineteenth-Century American Colleges*. Paper. NCTE.

And numerous articles. Additional books may be required reading.

Syllabus, Short Form

First Week: Introduction to Course, detailing what will be covered in the seminar and how it will be covered, etc.

We will spend some time—though ever so briefly—establishing an 'academic' context with which JB 'thought about' writing instruction. This context was primarily established for him while participating in a nine-month NEH seminar at Carnegie-Mellon University (1978–1979) with Richard Young. Specifically, we will examine some of the initial conceptual starting places that JB studied: Daniel Fogarty's notion of "Current-Traditional Rhetoric" (CTR), James Kinneavy's theories (rather, topologies) of discourse, and Young's topology of writing theory/instruction.

I will distribute selections from: Daniel Fogarty's *Roots for a New Rhetoric*. New York: Teachers College, Columbia U, 1959. I will briefly discuss several other articles that you will have read for next week, including my introductory article on JB in *Twentieth-Century Rhetorics and Rhetoricians*.

Lecture/Discussion Notes, Week #1

Continuing to establish the academic context, we will discuss the following two articles that JB first wrote while an NEH Fellow and published shortly thereafter (with Robert P. Inkster): "Current-Traditional Rhetoric: Paradigm and Practice." *Freshman English News* 8.3 (Winter 1980): 1–4, 13–14.

"Richard Whately and Current-Traditional Rhetoric." *College English* 42 (September 1980): 10–17.

Supplementary reading, which is necessary for a contextual interpretation:

Richard E. Young, "Paradigms and Problems: Needed Research in Rhetorical Invention." In *Research on Composing: Points of Departure*, Ed. Charles R. Cooper and Lee Odell. Urbana, IL: NCTE, 1978. 29–48.

—. "Arts, Crafts, Gifts and Knacks: Some Disharmonies in the New Rhetoric." In *Reinventing the Rhetorical Tradition*. Ed. Aviva Freedman and Ian Pringle. Conway, AK: Canadian Council of Teachers of English and L&S Books, 1980. 53–60.

VjV's Lecture/Discussion Notes, Week #2

September 8th: JB's first major article and its impact on theorizing and teaching writing instructions:

"Contemporary Composition: The Major Pedagogical Theories." *College English* 44 (1982): 765–77.

Supplementary reading, which is necessary for a contextual interpretation:

Richard Fulkerson, "Four Philosophies of Composition." CCC 30 (December 1979): 343–48.

Paul Kameen, "Rewording the Rhetoric of Composition." *PRE/TEXT* 1. 1–2 (Spring-Fall 1980). 3–94. Though Kameen was not a member of the seminar, he attended and participated. His article was available in draft form previous to publication and was read by JB and acknowledged in the *College English* article.

VjV's Lecture/Discussion Notes, Week #3

The First Book: *Writing Instruction in Nineteenth-Century American Colleges*. Carbondale, Southern Illinois UP, 1984.

Supplementary Reading

"Rhetoric and Poetics in the English Department: Our Nineteenth-Century Inheritance." *College English* 47 (1985): 531–33.

Connors, Robert J. Rev. of *Writing Instruction in Nineteenth-Century American Colleges*, James A. Berlin. *College Composition and Communications* 37 (1986): 247–49.

VjV's Lecture/Discussion Notes, Week #4

The Second Book: *Rhetoric and Reality: Writing Instruction in American Colleges.*1900–1985. Carbondale: Southern Illinois UP, 1987.

Supplementary Reading

Crowley, Sharon. Rev of *Rhetoric and Reality: Writing Instruction in American Colleges*: 1900–1985, James A. Berlin. *College Composition and Communication* 39 (1986): 245–47.

VjV's Lecture/Discussion Notes, Week #5

Historiography, Part 1

"Revisionary History: The Dialectical Method." *PRE/TEXT* 8.1–2 (1987): 47–61.
Berlin, James A., et al. Octalog. "The Politics of Historiography." *Rhetoric Review* 7 (1988): 5–49.
"Postmodernism, Politics, and Histories of Rhetorics." *PRE/TEXT*, 11.3–4 (1990): 169–87.

Supplementary Reading

Brooks, Kevin. "Reviewing and Re-describing 'The Politics of Historiography': Octalog I, 1988." *Rhetoric Review* 16.1 (Fall 1997): 6–21. In the same issue, you will find Octalog II. I do recommend that you eventually read this follow up event(less).

VjV's Lecture/Discussion Notes, Week #6

October 6th: JB's second major article and its impact on theorizing and teaching writing instructions:

"Rhetoric and Ideology in the Writing Class." *College English* 50 (1988): 477–94.

Supplementary Reading

Flower, Linda. "Comments on James Berlin. 'Rhetoric and Ideology in the Writing Class.'" *College English* 51 (1989): 765–69.
Schilb, John. "Comments on James Berlin. 'Rhetoric and Ideology in the Writing Class.'" *College English* 51 (1989): 769–70.
Scriben, Karen. "Comments on James Berlin. 'Rhetoric and Ideology in the Writing Class.'" *College English* 51 (1989): 764–65.
"James Berlin Responds. 'Rhetoric and Ideology in the Writing Class.'" *College English* 51 (1989): 770–77.

VjV's Lecture/Discussion Notes, Week #7

Historiography, Part 2

"Revisionary Histories of Rhetoric: Politics, Power, and Plurality." *Writing Histories of Rhetoric*, ed. Victor J. Vitanza. Carbondale: Southern Illinois UP, 1994. 112–27.

Supplementary reading:

Sharon Crowley, "Let Me Get This Straight." In Writing Histories of Rhetoric. Ed. Victor J. Vitanza. Carbondale: Southern Illinois UP, 1994. 20–37.

Hans Kellner, "After the Fall: Reflections on Histories of Rhetoric." In Writing Histories of Rhetoric. Ed. Victor J. Vitanza. Carbondale: Southern Illinois UP, 1994. 38–48.

VjV's Lecture/Discussion Notes, Week #8

Cultural Studies, Part 1

"Cultural Studies." *Encyclopedia of Rhetoric and Composition*. Ed. Theresa Enos. NY: Garland, 1996. 154–56.

"Freirean Pedagogy in the U.S.: A Response." *Journal of Advanced Composition* 12 (Fall 1992): 414–21.

"Poststructuralism, Cultural Studies, and the Composition Classroom." *Rhetoric Review* 11 (Fall 1992): 16–33. Rpt. *Professing the New Rhetorics: A Sourcebook*. Ed. Theresa Enos and Stuart C. Brown. Englewood Cliffs, New Jersey: Prentice Hall, 1994. 461–80.

VjV's Lecture/Discussion Notes, Week #9

Cultural Studies, Part 2

"Composition and Cultural Studies." *Composition and Resistance*. Ed. Hurlbert, C. Mark and Michael Blitz. Portsmouth, NH: Boynton/Cook, 1991.

"Composition Studies and Cultural Studies: Collapsing Boundaries." *Into the Field: Sites of Composition Studies*. Ed. Anne Ruggle Gere. New York: MLA,1993. 99–116.

Supplementary Reading

Bizzell, Patricia. "Beyond anti-Foundationalism Rhetorical Authority: Problems Defining 'Cultural Literacy.'" *College English* 52.6 (1990): 661–75. (Critique of Berlin on pp. 670, 672–673)

Notice that this article is published much earlier than the articles we read this week, but it's a critique that stands with value and that raises important questions that we should wrestle with.

VjV's Lecture/Discussion Notes, Week #10

A Major Interrogation of JB's Work

Alcorn, Marshall. "Changing the Subject of Postmodernist Theory: Discourse, Ideology, and Therapy in the Classroom." *Rhetoric Review* 13.2 (1995): 331–49.

Note: JB, as an outside reviewer, had read the manuscript of this article and had sent his comments to the editor of *Rhetoric Review*. The notes, published posthumously, are included along with the article. Some background in Lacanian psychoanalysis will be necessary to follow the argument.

VjV's Lecture/Discussion Notes, Week #11

The Final Book, published posthumously.

Rhetorics, Poetics, and Cultures: Refiguring College English Studies. Urbana, IL: NCTE, 1996. (Republished with an Afterword by Janice Lauer and Response Essays by Linda Brodkey, Patricia Harkin, Susan Miller, John Trimbur, and Victor J. Vitanza by Parlor Press, 2003).

Supplementary Reading

"Jim Berlin's Last Work: Future Perfect, Tense" (A collection of articles by Linda Brodkey, Patricia Harkin, Susan Miller, John Trimbur, and Victor J. Vitanza on Rhetorics, Poetics, Cultures). *Journal of Advanced Composition* 17.3 (1997): 489–505.

VjV's Lecture/Discussion Notes, Week #12-13

A Retrospective

Seminar participants (taking as reading course for exams/dissertation) will have composed a two-page summary of their positions vis-a-vis Berlin's theories/pedagogies of writ instruction and their own, emphasizing what they have incorporated and/or disincorporated, and present it to the seminar.

Syllabus, Long Form

Week #1

Notes used for 25 Aug 1998 Seminar Meeting. —vjv

Introduction to Seminar: Beginning with Maps or Topologies or Cartographic Representations of Rhetoric/Composition.

Context, NEH Seminar (AY 1978–79): What is included here are Maps or Topologies for the most part given to us in lecture format by **Richard Young** or shared among us outside of the NEH Seminar and known or used in part by JB in articles shortly after the seminar. The maps—cognitive mappings—were used as a means of orienting the NEH participants to the field of rhetoric/composition:

- Daniel Fogarty's divisions (roots for a new rhetoric): Aristotle, Current Traditional, Newer Theories (Richards, Burke, General Semanticists)

> **Historical Note:** Daniel John Fogarty, S.J., was the Dean of Education at St. Mary's, Canada, in the 50s through the 70s. The on-line archives at St. Mary's have little information other than to say he designed the university's crest and motto.
>
> The library has a second book entitled **A proposed inner college for Saint Mary's University** Halifax: Institute for the Study of Values, Saint Mary's University, 1969. I am writing the public relations office at St. Mary's to get additional information. We know very little about Fogarty, the person whose book (roots for a new rhetoric) we often use.

- James Kinneavy's topologies of discourse (theory of discourse): Expressive, Persuasive, Referential, Literary

- Frank D'Angelo's topics/topologies of discourse (a conceptual theory of rhetoric): Logical (Static, Progressive, Repetitive) and Nonlogical (Imagining, condensation, symbolizing, displacement, free association, transformation, nonlogical repetition), etc. (See **A Conceptual Theory of Rhetoric**. Cambridge, Mass.: Winthrop, 1975.)
- Hal Rivers Weidner (doctoral dissertation): Traditional, Mechanical, and Vital. (This dissertation—"Three Models of Rhetoric: Traditional, Mechanical and Vital," U of Michigan, 1975—was read by members of the NEH seminar. The model of Vitalism is applied to Romanticism, specifically Coleridge, and then later "The New Romantics." See Kameen's Article in Syllabus, third week, September 8th.)

> **Note:** See Kinneavy's article "A Pluralistic Synthesis of Four Contemporary Models for Teaching Composition" in **Reinventing the Rhetorical Tradition**. Ed. Aviva Freedman and Ian Pringle. Conway, AR: CCTE and L&S Books, 1980. 37–52. (K compares and gives a plural synthesis of Moffett, Britton, Kinneavy, and D'Angelo.)

- Stephen C. Pepper's Root Metaphors (world hypotheses): formalism, mechanism, organicism, and contextualism
- Northrop Frye's Mythoi (anatomy of criticism): comedy, romance, tragedy, and irony (satire)
- M. H. Abrams's Metaphors (the mirror and the lamp): Pragmatic, Mimetic, Expressive, Objective.

> **Note:** See Richard Fulkerson, in "Four Philosophies of Composition." CCC 30 [December 1979]: 343–48. Pragmatic, Mimetic, Expressive, Objective... became for RF... Rhetorical, Mimetic, Expressive, Formalist. (RF's article in CCC was not available during the time of the NEH seminar, but JB responded to it in his "Contemporary Composition.")

> **Note:** Weidner opens his discussion with tipping his hat ("I owe a debt" [iv]) to Abrams's *The Mirror and the Lamp*.

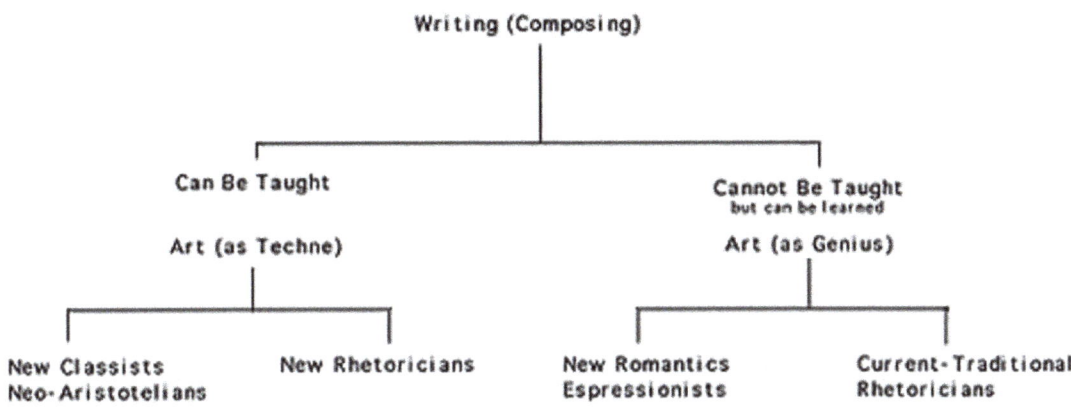

Chart 1, Topology given by Richard Young during NEH Seminar, Fall, 1978

The question here is whether or not writing can be taught. There is a certain amount of confusion in using the word "ART." Young, therefore, made the following division to clarify the confusion: There is **art as techne** and **art as "art" produced by genius**. It is basically assumed that art as techne (dynamism) can be taught because the act of creating or solving problems is **generic**, not unique, and therefore can be **codified** and **taught**. It is basically assumed that art as genius cannot be taught, but learned, because the act of creating or solving problems is unique (nonrational) and therefore cannot be codified and taught.

The generic attributes that are codified can and have been developed into algorithic procedures, heuristic procedures, and aleatory procedures.

> **Art as Techne:** New Classicists, neo-Aristotelians. Examples would be Corbett and his *Classical Rhetoric for the Modern Student*. New Rhetoricians. Examples would be Burke and Young, Becker, and Pike.
>
> **Art as Genius:** Current-Traditional Rhetoricians. Examples would be Genung. The New Romantics (a.k.a. Expressionists). Examples would be Murray, Elbow, Coles.

John Genung (CTR) has written that interventional procedures, rhetorical capacities, techne/dynamism, "though very real and valuable, are not practical because the ability to employ them cannot be imparted by teaching. They have to exist in the writer himself, in the peculiar bent of his nature.

> . . . All the work of origination must be left to the writer himself; the rhetorical text-book can merely treat of those mental habits and power which give firmness and system to his suggestive faculty. . . . The first stage, the finding of material by thought or observation, is the fundamental and inclusive office of invention, the distinctive power that we designate in the popular use of the term. Herein lies obviously the heart and center of literary production; it is what the writer finds, in his subject or in the world of thought, that gauges his distinction as an author. Yet this is, of all processes, the one least to be invaded by the rules of the text-book. It is a work so individual, so dependent on the peculiar aptitude and direction of the writer's mind, that each one must be left for the most part to find his way alone, according to the impulse that is in him."

In John Genung, **The Practical Elements of Rhetoric**. 1892. xi, 8, 217. (These passages as well as the book were read by the NEH Fellows. . . . Young was at the time working on the article "Arts, Crafts, Gifts and Knacks: Some Disharmonies in the New Rhetoric," in which he quotes these passages.)

William E. Coles, Jr (New Romantic) has written:

> The fact is that the teaching of writing as writing is the teaching of writing as art. When writing is not taught as art, as more than a craft or a skill, it is not writing that is being taught, but something else. To teach writing as something else, to teach art as non-art, is to make impossible the conception of art as art. On the other hand, art because it is art, cannot be taught. What is wanted then, for the teaching of writing as writing, is a way of teaching what cannot be taught, a course to make possible what no course can do. (*The Plural I—and After*)

In William E. Coles, Jr., **The Plural I—and After**. Portsmouth, NH: Boynton/Cook and Heinemann, 1988. (The first edition of this book was read by JB in the NEH seminar. Coles, who taught at the U of Pittsburgh, visited the seminar and discussed issues with the participants.)

Richard Young (New Rhetorician) has written:

> What is taught? The answer is 'heuristics,' that is, explicit strategies for effective guessing. Heuristic procedures are not to be confused with rule-governed procedures; for if we fail to make the distinction, we end by rejecting the use of explicit techniques in composing since there are few rule-governed procedures possible in rhetoric. A rule-governed procedure specifies a finite series of steps that can be carried out consciously and mechanically without the aid of intuition or special ability, and if properly carried out always yields a correct result. . . . On the other hand, a heuristic procedure provides a series of questions or operations whose results are provisional. Although explicit and more or less systematic, heuristic search is not

wholly conscious or mechanical; intuition, relevant knowledge, and skill are also necessary. ("Arts, Crafts, Gifts and Knacks" 57)

> **Historical Note:** Of great importance is the exchange in **CCC** during the early 1970s between Janice Lauer and Ann E. Berthoff over heuristics and composition: See Lauer, "Heuristics and Composition"; Berthoff, "The Problem of Problem Solving"; Lauer, "The Problem of Problem Solving"; Berthoff, "Counterstatement." This exchange has been collected in W. Ross Winterowd's **Contemporary Rhetoric: A Conceptual Background with Readings**. NY: Harcourt Brace Jovanovich, 1975. 79–103. (This exchange was studied in the NEH seminar.)

Week #2

Notes Used for 1 Sept 1998 Seminar Meeting. —vjv

Continuing to establish the academic context (NEH Seminar, AY1978-79)

Richard Young had us read his article "Paradigms and Problems" during the first couple of weeks. The article functioned as a map of the entire first semester of the seminar, which was on rhetorical invention (the second semester was on the composing process): Young opens with re-establishing Kuhn's notion of the paradigm, which was well known by members of the seminar, for it had been used previously and widely in many disciplines.

> Richard E. Young, "Paradigms and Problems: Needed Research in Rhetorical Invention." In **Research on Composing: Points of Departure**, Ed. Charles R. Cooper and Lee Odell. Urbana, IL: NCTE, 1978. 29–48.

Young begins with Fogarty's view of current-traditional rhetoric (CTR) and then describes "Vitalism" (31). Note that Young sites Weidner and Kantor. (Again, the NEH Fellows read—JB definitely read—Weidner's depiction of Vitalism, which was almost solely in terms of Coleridge; I don't remember our being given a copy of Kantor's dissertation or anyone talking about it.)

Young writes,

> The main difficulty in discussing the current-traditional paradigm, or even in recognizing its existence, is that so much of our theoretical knowledge about it is tacit [allusion to Polanyi]. Such is the case with the vitalistic assumptions, inherited from the Romantics, that underlie so many of its overt features [e.g.,] the emphasis on the composed product rather than the composing process; the analysis of discourse into words, sentences, and paragraphs; the classification of discourse into description, narration, exposition, and argument; the

> strong concern with usage (syntax, spelling, punctuation) and with style (economy, clarity, emphasis); the preoccupation with the informal essay and the research paper.... (31)

This statement, which is oft quoted is filled with paraphrases. The talk here about the Vitalists and the Romantics is from Weidner; the description of CTR step by step is, of course, from Fogarty. As best as I can tell, Young was the first in rhetoric and composition **to conflate** the two (Vitalism + CTR) together.

I am making much of this point for two reasons: (1) A few of the NEH Fellows felt uneasy about the conflation, for we did not accept Weidner's thesis, and (2) JB wrote shortly after the seminar against this conflation. As far as I know, JB is the only person among us who wrote *at length* against Weidner's view of Coleridge, as the archetypal Romantic, and his being linked to CTR and Vitalism. (More about this point later.)

It's important to know that there were other attitudes being expressed about the Romantics. It is the case that, e.g., Frank D'Angelo (in **A Conceptual Theory of Rhetoric**, 1975) was talking favorably at times about the 'new Romantics' and specifically in terms of composition theory/pedagogy. He writes:

> The emphasis on creative expression and on personal writing in Great Britain and in the United States in recent years suggests additional roles for both teacher and students. This kind of writing seems to be directly related to the contemporary interest in exploring alternate modes of consciousness. The impetus for such exploration seems to derive, at least in part, from Freudian and Jungian psychology and from humanistic and existential approaches to human behavior by such psychologists as Rollo May, Abraham Maslow, Carl Rogers, and R. D. Laing. The importance of these new approaches is that they provide a healthy balance to the rational, systematic approaches to writing which have long dominated the classroom. These new approaches emphasize feeling rather than intellect, exploration and discovery rather than preconceived ideas, the imagination, creativity, free association, fantasy, play, dreams, the un-couscous, nonintellectual sensing, the stream-of-consciousness, and the self. (*Conceptual* 159)

D'Angelo goes on to establish an outline for a new set of topoi for these alternate modes. It is important to know and to keep in mind that D'Angelo wrote: "This new emphasis on writing which is relatively free of control and direction may be termed the new romanticism" (*Conceptual* 159).

There is, no doubt, however, eventually in the minds of most theoreticians and practitioners that the Romantics are to be blamed for the exclusion of invention (the principle of origination) from Rhetoric and writing instruction. And there is not too much doubt by commentators that the German and British Romantics were specifically to blame. The literature on this subject is easily available; in composition, see Sharon Crowley, **The Methodical Memory: Invention in Current-Traditional Rhetoric**, which some of us read and discussed in E5353, Spring 1997; and read Ross Winterowd, **The English Department**, especially ch. 2, "Discovery—>Invention<—Creation." There is always a **clash** between the systematic and the nonsystematic (*ingenium**).

Perhaps I should not go without saying that there were, of course, other previous and later forces and characters at work in history, such as Ramus and B Croce, who greatly diminished the value of invention, and besides Romanticism (the so-called Vitalist model) there was the Mechanistic model. Though important, these are other narratives, while ours focuses on the Young's article "Paradigms and Problems." (I will furnish you with a few additional citations, if you wish, especially in respect to the history of rhetoric; those of you who took HUMA 5301from me read some of this literature.)

*Cf. **ingegno**, the power of conceiving, judging, reasoning; the faculty that can transport us from one thing to the next. (See R.Barilli, *Rhetoric* Ch. 5. Minnesota: U of Minneapolis, 1989.)

This **clash** can be used and has been used in inventive ways! (JB will develop the clash in terms of dialectical exchanges when he begins to write about ideology.)

Once Young conflates Widner + Fogarty in his "Paradigms and Problems," he then goes on to talk about a crisis. Which is CTR's "failure to provide effective instruction in what is often called the 'prewriting stage' of the composing process and in the analytical and synthetic skills necessary for good thinking" (33).

At this point in the article, Young lists what he calls "four substantial theories of invention" (35):

- Classical Invention
- Burke's Dramatistic Method
- Rohman's Prewriting Method
- Pike's Tagmemic Invention

We (JB) studied invention in these four portions, with Young placing special emphasis on the latter.

After reading "Paradigms and Problems," we began to work our way through the various articles listed and described in Young's bibliographical article "Invention: A Topographical Survey" in **Teaching Composition: 10 Bibliographical Essays**. Fort Worth, TX: TCU P, 1976. 1–44. In addition, we initially spent an appropriate amount of time on the doctrines of *stasis* or *status*.

What I am trying to stress here—as I stated in last week's notes and at the beginning of this week's notes—is the overall context in which Invention was presented in the NEH Seminar and the important fact that while JB takes much of what R. Young introduced and taught us, JB questions, in part, Young's acceptance of Weidner's claim about Coleridge.

In his article "Richard Whately and Current-Traditional Rhetoric" (1980) he differs with Young. (See later discussion in these notes.) But JB is most convincing in his article "The Rhetoric of Romanticism" (1980), which I have not assigned, but will put on reserve. JB writes:

> One significant reason for misunderstanding Coleridge's rhetoric is that seeing it for what it is requires the proper historical perspective. Coleridge is not an Aristotelian; he does not, for example, think of rhetoric as the art of discovering the available means of persuasion, with the emphasis on inventional devices that this view implies. At the same time, his rhetoric does not belong to the eighteenth-century and its focus on the effects of discourse on the audience. (In fact, the conflation of Coleridge with the eighteenth-century rhetorics of Smith and Blair has, I am convinced, led Young and Weidner astray.) This, of course, is hard to recognize since the eighteenth century itself led a profound revolution in the conception of rhetoric which was in many ways anti-Aristotelian. Coleridge's rhetoric, on the other hand—like his thought in general—develops out of his fervid disagreement with the metaphysic, poetic, and rhetoric of the previous century. In turning his back on the tradition of Aristotle as well as his inheritance from the eighteenth-century, Coleridge turns to Plato and Plato's modern counterparts in Germany. (James A. Berlin. "The Rhetoric of Romanticism." *Rhetoric Society Quarterly,* Spring 1980, 62–74)

What is especially evident in this 1980 article is JB's acceptance of Coleridge in terms of the thinker's love of dialectic as method. JB sees Coleridge as a Platonist, and yet a 'Platonist' who views **Poetry** (poetics) and **Rhetoric** as being equally valuable in a dialectical exchange. JB in a few years will include leftist Hegelian dialectic as a heuristic in his discussions of historiography and cultural studies.

We will take a look at this article on Romanticism next time (see syllabus, week #3) and will read it along with Paul Kameen's article on the value of Coleridge. (As will become clear soon, Kameen sat in on Young's NEH seminar but also was a later Fellow in Ann Berthoff's summer NEH seminar! Ah, we are growing dialectically!)

The linkage between CRT and Vitalism is still generally accepted to this day. Most recently, Ross Winterowd, in his "Prologue" to **The English Department: A Personal and Institutional History** (Carbondale: SIUP, 1998) goes on at length discussing Ann Berthoff's acceptance of Coleridge and in the subsequent chapters of the book literature departments' acceptance of Romanticism and the negative impact such an acceptance has had on the teaching of writing in departments of literature (English).

Before taking a look at the second article by Young, Let's examine another topology that Young gave the NEH Fellows, a topology that complements our discussion last week about the three kinds of discovery procedures: algorithmic, heuristic, and aleatory.

> "*Glamour* and *grammar* or, in French, *grimoire* and *grammaire* were originally the same word and thus combined, even in the vocabulary, the magical and rationalistic aspect of speech." —Jacqueline de Romilly, *Magic and Rhetoric in Ancient Greece* (v).

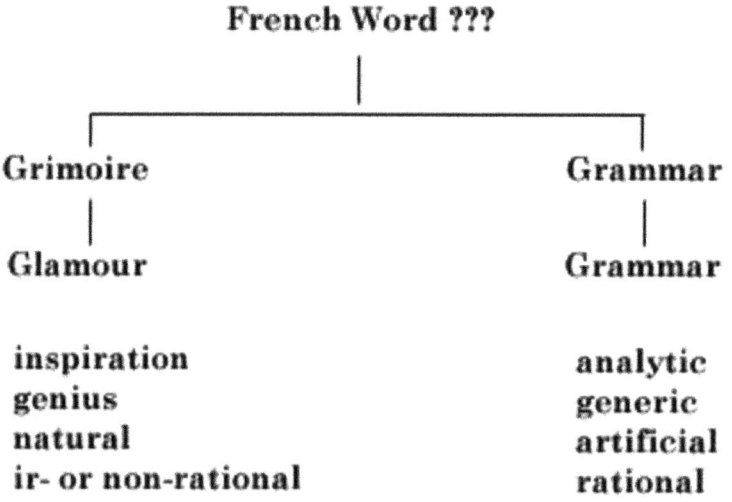

Chart 2, Topology of grimoire and grammar given by Richard Young during NEH Seminar, Fall, 1978

This topology, like the previous one, must not be read algorithmically, but heuristically. The topology, in other words, is an aid to reflection. What Young is suggesting, by way of de Romilly, is that there was a uniformity (perhaps) . . . one can project such a uniformity, though the French word (???) in this case is no longer known . . . a uniformity between **magic** (spells) and **rhetoric** (say, informal logic). Or between **poetry** and **rhetoric**. Gorgias, as de Romilly points out, uses ancient magic in his poetic rhetoric. Young said that it would do us well to ponder this split and yet potential uniformity. (Recall, as stated above, JB's interest in combining and seeing as co-equal both poetry and rhetoric in Coleridge.)

> "Arts, Crafts, Gifts and Knacks: Some Disharmonies in the New Rhetoric." In **Reinventing the Rhetorical Tradition.** Ed. Aviva Freedman and Ian Pringle. Conway, AK: Canadian Council of Teachers of English and L&S Books, 1980.

The second article by Young was not read by the NEH Fellows but Young was working on it at the time and much that he says in the article was given to us in lecture form.

The article begins with the above quote from de Romilly. The article is an examination of the split between magic and rhetoric and how it manifests itself historically in the 18th through the 20th centuries. The split contributes to what in the subtitle Young refers to as "Disharmonies in the New Rhetoric." I don't want to spend too much time on the article, for I think it is an easy enough one to read, especially in the light of what we have said and thus far read. The statement that best sums up Young's purpose in the article is his speaking of "apparently two irreconcilable positions" (55). Again, recall the topology above based on de Romilly (magic and rhetoric). Young writes:

> **Historical Note:** Young delivered this paper at the Canadian Council of Teachers of English Conference in May, 1979. The conference was held at Carleton University. (A number of NEH Fellows participated in this conference; JB did not attend.)

> One of these positions has been called the 'new romanticism.' The term is Frank D'Angelo's.... Though we lack the historical studies that permit generalizing with confidence, the position seems not so much an innovation in the discipline as a reaffirmation of the vitalist philosophy of an old romanticism enriched by modern psychology. It maintains that the composing process is, or should be, relatively free of deliberate control; that intellect is no more in touch with reality than non-logical processes; and that the act of composing is a kind of mysterious growth fed by what Henry James called 'the deep well of the unconscious cerebration' . . . The new romanticism presents the teacher of composition with a difficult problem (i.e., how does one teach a mystery?). William Coles makes the point well when he says that 'the teaching of writing as writing is the teaching of writing as art. When writing is not taught as art, as more than a craft or a skill, it is not writing that is being taught, but something else. . . . On the other hand, art because it is art, cannot be taught.' . . . Like Genung, Coles believes . . ." (55).

Young continues:

> The primary difference between the new romantics and those representing the second position I want to discuss, those we might call, for want of a better term, the 'new classicists,' is a difference in what constitutes an art. For the new romantics, art contrasts with craft: the craft of writing refers to skill in technique, or what Genung called 'mechanics,' a skill which can be taught. Art, on the other hand, is associated with more mysterious powers which may be enhanced but which are, finally, unteachable. Art as magic, as glamour.

For the new classicists, art means something quite different: it means the knowledge necessary for producing preconceived results by conscious, directed action. As such, it contrasts not with craft but with knack (i.e., a habit acquired through repeated experience). An art, for the new classicist, is the result of an effort to isolate and generalize what those who have knacks do when they are successful . . . (55, 56).

Young goes on to remind us that Aristotle attempted to isolate and generalize what those who have knacks actually do when successful.

Young (as new classicist, new rhetorician) says in response to the problem of What is to be taught? How is one to confront the mysteriousness of language.

> The answer is 'heuristics,' that is, explicit strategies for effective guessing. Heuristic procedures are not to be confused with rule-governed procedures; for if we fail to make the distinction, we end by rejecting the use of explicit techniques in composing since there are few rule-governed procedures possible in rhetoric. A rule-governed procedure specifies a finite series of steps that can be carried out consciously and mechanically without the aid of intuition or special ability, and if properly carried out always yields a correct result. . . . On the other hand, a heuristic procedure provides a series of questions or operations whose results are provisional. Although explicit and more or less systematic, heuristic search is not wholly conscious or mechanical; intuition, relevant knowledge, and skill are also necessary. (57)

With this background in mind, let's turn now to the first two Berlin articles:

In the first article (with Robert P. Inkster), "Current-Traditional Rhetoric: Paradigm and Practice" (**Freshman English News** 8. 3 (Winter 1980): 1–4, 13–14), we can see, if not hear, a number of obvious echoes.

What JB and RI do is to examine and further develop what Young had taught them. They take a number of textbooks in the field and clearly demonstrate that CTR dominates the available textbooks for teachers of writing.

During the seminar and in between discussions of the four new methods of invention, Young brought in textbook after textbook (Strunk and White, **Elements of Style**; S. Baker, **The Practical Stylist**, etc.) and taught us how to read them in terms of his basic topologies. In many cases in contemporary textbooks, there was touted in the title or the TOC the buzz word "process"; all the texts, however, were clearly CTR.

JB and RI read the textbooks semiotically across the communications triangle. I don't mean to suggest here that theirs was a mechanical exercise based on what they learned in the NEH seminar; on the contrary, what JB and RI do, as any good thinker will do at this point in time, is to further verify and demonstrate the thesis of the crisis: Namely, that we are still in the midst of CTR and we must, in this case, develop and write better, more appropriate texts based on recent research done by 'new rhetoricians.' Many others were to further verify this thesis to initiate some changes.

In the second article ("Richard Whately and Current-Traditional Rhetoric." **College English** 42 [September 1980]: 10–17), JB continues his development of Fogarty-Young's claim about CTR, while questioning Weidner-Young's claim about vitalism. He writes: "In attributing to Blair rather than to English Romantics, such as Coleridge, the source of the vitalist theory of creation in current-traditional rhetoric, I differ with Young . . . and with Hal Rivers Weidner . . . (13, n11).

JB points out from the beginning of the article that nothing has been done on Whately and that he hopes "to show that Whately's **Elements** served as a prototype for the textbooks written by Genung and Hill, which in turn shaped our modern college rhetorics. To get to this point, JB works from his mentor's description of CTR (10–11). Finally, he makes the following points:

That Whately

- offers "a new inventio of management to replace the classical inventio of discovery" (this characterization, JB takes from Ehninger);

That Whately's

- "departures from Aristotle are more significant than his similarities" (this he determines by claiming Whately depicts rhetoric as an "off-shoot" instead of a "counterpart" of logic/dialectic . . . but this statement is partially problematic, for Aristotle himself uses both metaphors of 'off-shoot' and 'counterpart,' but I think it's correct to accept the notion that Aristotle deemed rhetoric a counterpart and that Whately went in the opposite direction, taking invention as an offshoot and then out of the canon altogether);

That Whately's

- instructions for writing fit precisely Fogarty's description of CTR (or, I should say, Fogarty's description of CTR fit precisely Whately's advice on how to write);

That Whately's

- discussion of argument and persuasion is worth our reading Whately, but that we need to realize and act on the knowledge that our view of the composing process is today (1980) "based on a model designed in 1828." JB concludes: "Whether or not a rhetoric devised for the first third of the nineteenth century is still adequate today ought to be considered." And then in what will be characteristic of JB's later mature interrogations, he ends the article: "Have we taken too uncritically the assurances of Whately, Hill, Genung, and their contemporary counter-parts that they offer not *a* rhetoric but *the* rhetoric, eternal and true? I.A. Richards, Kenneth Burke, Richard Young, Richard Ohmann, and numerous others think that indeed we have and that it is time for a reassessment. It is in the spirit of their work that I offer this attempt at understanding our history and our practice" (17). JB is very politic as he lays the groundwork for moving out eventually on his own!

Week #3

Notes Used for 8 Sept 1998 Seminar Meeting. —vjv

Continuing to establish the academic context (NEH Seminar, AY1978-79) |||| JB's first major article and its impact on theorizing and teaching writing instructions:

> "Contemporary Composition: The Major Pedagogical Theories." **College English** 44 (1982): 765–77.

In discussing JB's first major article we will continue to look at some of the influences that originate from the NEH Seminar and will begin to take note of how JB is developing his own sense of what it is that he wants to say. He emphatically differs in political terms from Richard Fulkerson ("Four Philosophies of Composition." **CCC** 30 [December 1979]: 343–48) and agrees with Kameen ("Re-wording the Rhetoric of Composition." **PRE/TEXT** 1.1–2 [Spring-Fall 1980]. 73–94).

First, let's take a look at Fulkerson's map of the field (universe) of discourse and then a look at Kameen's and finally how JB disagrees with Fulkerson's finding nothing wrong with expressive discourse and how he extends and reconfigures Kameen's map in order to put forth his map and groupings with each category and to put forth his political views in respect to each category.

It is important to remember that Kameen sat in on the NEH seminar and is responding directly to much that Young said in print and in seminar and that seminarians read, specifically, Weidner's depiction of Coleridge and the notion of Vitalism. Note that Kameen cites JB's "The Rhetoric of Romanticism: The Case for Coleridge."

> **Historical Note and Humorous Detail:** When JB had his article accepted, he called and told me about his success and mentioned that the editor had asked him why he bothered to cite Kameen's article since it was published in **PRE/TEXT**. He recalled that the editor asked, "Who reads PRE/TEXT?," to which Jim responded, "People who do their homework!" A few years later, Jim quipped, "49 PRE/TEXT Readers can't be wrong!," which became the journal's motto.

Fulkerson selects Abrams's category system (map, configuration) to illustrate a very important point, namely, that many teachers of writing assign a discourse type and then assess it by way of a contradictory type.

Abram's Categories (According to Fulkerson)

Pragmatic ("Any theory making the reader primary, and judging literature by its effect, Abrams labels *pragmatic*");

Mimetic ("When the universe shared by artist and auditor becomes the primary element and measure of success, then, Abrams says, we have a *mimetic* theory, such as that of Pope and the Neo-Classical period");

Expressive ("Emphasis on the personal views of the artist, such as in the Romantic period, Abrams labels the *exspressive* position");

Objective ("...theories emphasizing only the internal relationships within the artifact, Abrams calls *objective* criticism").

Fulkerson's Appropriation and Renaming of the Categories

- *Pragmatic* becomes **Rhetorical**
- *Mimetic* stays **Mimetic**
- *Expressive* stays **Expressive**
- *Objective* becomes **Formalist**

Fulkerson writes: "I will keep the term *expressive* for philosophies of composition emphasizing the writer and the term *mimetic* for philosophies emphasizing correspondence with 'reality.' But philosophies emphasizing the effect on a reader I will call *rhetorical*, and philosophies emphasizing traits internal to the work I will call *formalist*."

Kameen's Categories Appropriation

Fulkerson's thesis:

> . . . this four-part perspective helps give a coherent view of what goes on in composition classes. All four philosophies exist in practice. They give rise to vastly different ways of judging student writing, vastly different courses to lead students to produce such writing, vastly different textbooks and journal articles. Moreover, the perspective helps to clarify, though not to resolve, a number of the major controversies in the field, including the "back-to-the-basics" cry and the propriety of dialectical variations in student writing.

Fulkerson points out how the *four* categories are in line with Kinneavy's persuasive, reference, expressive, and literary aims.

Having established his four philosophies, Fulkerson adds:

> My research has convinced me that in many cases composition teachers either fail to have a consistent value theory or fail to let that philosophy shape pedagogy. . . . [T]hey are guilty of mindlessness. A fairly common writing assignment . . . directs the student to 'state and explain clearly your opinion about X.' . . . **There is nothing wrong with such an assignment.** But if a student does state his or her opinion and if the opinion happens to be based on gross ignorance or to contain major contradictions, the teacher must, to be consistent, ignore such matters. The topic as stated asks for opinion; it does not ask for good opinion, judged by whatever philosophy. In short, the assignment implies an expressive value-theory. It does not say, 'Express your opinion to persuade a reader' (which would imply a mimetic theory), or even 'Express your opinion correctly' (implying a formalist theory). To give the bald assignment and then judge it from any of the perspectives not implied is to be guilty of value-mode confusion. (emphasis added)

Again, Fulkerson claims: "**There is nothing wrong with an expressive philosophy**, but there is something seriously wrong with classroom methodology which implies one variety of value judgment when another will actually be employed. That is modal confusion, mindlessness" (emphasis added).

JB would—and does—say that there is something very wrong with the philosophy as well as with giving such an assignment. (We will return to this issue later after taking a look at Kameen's article.)

Kameen carefully read the same material that the seminarians read, especially Weidner's dissertation and Young's conflation of CTR and Coleridge's form of expressions as Vitalist. He attempts to extend JB's "The Rhetoric of Romanticism: The Case for Coleridge" but also attempts to develop *three* philosophies or "meta-rhetorical assumptions, both epistemological and linguistic" (73) about composition theory and pedagogy. While Kameen accepts the category of expressivism-vitalism, he argues against Coleridge as being vitalist. He sees, instead, Coleridge, like JB does, as maintaining a dialectical balance between self and world. Let's take a closer look at Kameen's attempt:

Like JB and Inkster before him—he cites them—Kameen writes: ". . . a composition textbook is not simply a pedagogical device for enabling students to improve their writing; it is also a definition of what writing is and what writing is for, a kind of argument whose surface rhetoric depends on a broad web of meta-rhetorical assumptions. . ." (73). Like Fulkerson, he stresses the "seemingly chaotic array of approaches [in textbooks] competing for our attention" (73). However, Kameen writes,

> a myriad of possibilities yields to an initial order. For there are three major foci around which most composition textbooks constellate, with each group depending on a different epistemic base of initiating discourse. These are (1) in the real, of forms, with particular emphasis on the abstract modes of thought that organize knowledge and discourse; (2) in the inner precincts of the self, with particular emphasis on experiential writing and authentic voices; and (3) in the domain of audience, with particular emphasis on writing as a heuristically-enabled, information-processing behavior. (73)

Immediately, these groupings and particular words inscribing them should echo familiar terms and phrases:

Kameen's Categories

- formalism (structuralism)
- self, expressionism
- audience

Kameen continues:

> . . . each of these categories is both created and bounded by certain metaphoric conceptions of the 'universe of discourse' within which writing can take place. Each inscribes itself within various sets of dichotomies—thought/feeling, form/content, expression/communication, self/audience, etc.—which constrain its field of inquiry. These parts, usually conceived as polar opposites rather than as dialectical contraries, constitute the channels along which

> that approach issues. On a more concrete level, each is both created and bounded by the very particular metaphors that function as analogies for the writing process. One such metaphor is 'exploration,' which serves as a powerful symptomatic emblem of implicit assumptions concerning the nature and purpose of composition. (73–74)

The *first* of these (i.e., "in the real, of forms, with particular emphasis on the abstract modes of thought that organize knowledge and discourse" or formalism/structuralism) is found in Frank D'Angelo's work, specifically in his textbook **Process and Thought in Composition** and, as I mentioned during Week #2, in his theory book entitled **A Conceptual Theory of Rhetoric** for this textbook. Anyone familiar with D'Angelo's work knows that he posits the topoi as onto-genetic (as constants in thinking). Hence, Kameen's reference to "real" and "forms."

> **Historical Note:** D'Angelo is writing out of a Structuralist, Generative Grammar (Francis Christensen) and the Structuralist movement broadly defined (Piaget, Levy-Strauss, Foucault 1, Barthes 1, etc.), which was waning at the time of the seminar and being replaced by poststructuralist thought (Derrida, Foucault 2, Barthes 2, etc.). However, Bill Nelson, one of the NEH seminarians was a structuralist and argued for this position. See his article, published prior to the seminar, "Topoi: Evidence of Human Conceptual Behavior." In *Philosophy and Rhetoric* 2 (Winter 1969): 1–11. I went into the seminar as a Structuralist and came running out of it as a bloody, raving poststructuralist!

The *second* of these (i.e., "in the inner precincts of the self, with particular emphasis on experiential writing and authentic voices") is found in James E. Miller and Stephen Judy's *Writing in Reality*. Kameen agrees that Miller and Judy are working as expressionist and vitalists. He writes:

> Miller and Judy have delivered the writer out of the bondage of formal structures [content/form] which D'Angelo imposes over intentionality. Yet they have delivered him into an equally confining world wherein the motivation to write must arise mysteriously from 'inner sources.' . . . There is not then a great deal that we can actually teach about writing; for as Miller and Judy inform the student in their introduction, 'we feel no need to teach you about language. . . . You have the language; our aim is to help you release and control it.' . . . The implication is that the proper role of the instructor is simply to provide students with occasions for discourse and that they in turn will 'participate more actively, directly, and consciously in that creation of the self which is the major challenge of existence.' (76–77)

> **Humorous, Yet Sad Note:** Sam Watson, Jr., and I used to visit Bill Nelson occasionally and find him in his basement. He moved his professional stuff into the basement of the house that he and his family had rented in Pittsburgh. Bill would talk to us about going to garage sales with his wife and buying things and then talk to us very seriously, telling us time and again about Spinoza not writing but thinking. Just thinking! And while thinking, cutting and polishing lenses. Bill would pour another martini from his pitcher (reminding me later of KB) and just look at us, waiting for a response. When Bill was not in seminar, he was in his basement thinking. He was a very careful, processual thinker.
>
> The last that I heard from Bill was when he called me from his riverboat house. He had moved out of his family's house (where, I forget) and was just sitting on the deck looking out over the lake . . . thinking. Waiting for a thought, while he polished the rays bouncing off the surface of the lake. A month or so later, I heard that he had passed away. He knew—as he told me over the phone—that he had a 'heart condition.' He was the first to go.

The *third* of these (i.e., "in the domain of audience, with particular emphasis on writing as a heuristically-enabled, information-processing behavior") are the "new rhetorics" mentioned by Young, "which conceive of discourse not as an expression arising from the self but as a message focused toward an audience. These rhetorics are allied around a commitment to audience-based discourse, process models of composition, heuristic procedures for invention, and a general antagonism toward 'vitalism'" (78).

> **Caveat:** What is important to understand here—if someone comes to a reading and acceptance of JB's article "Contemporary Composition" prior to Kameen's article (putting des cartes before the horse)—is that Kameen is not setting up the category system of three concepts/things so as to determine and choose which one is the best or more politically acceptable view of reality for him. Kameen, instead, sets aside all three categories in an attempt to explain Coleridge and to ward off the conflation of Vitalism with Coleridgean Romanticism and to put forth a way out of the binaries or dichotomies (content/form, product/process, etc.) to **a tertiary process**.

> Therefore, again it is necessary to understand that though Kameen is looking at three, he is really looking at them individually and collectively across their self-imposed dichotomies. Such an understanding of what Kameen is doing will make for a different, eventually more interesting-productive rereading of JB's article and his later, mature thinking. Understand, therefore, that *my readings of Kameen and Berlin are that Kameen is more revolutionary in what he is saying at this point in time (1980) than what Berlin is saying, but that Berlin will eventually find another way of saying—and with very definite political terms and ends as 'tertiary processes.' Kameen did not continue to write; Jim could not stop writing and attempting to effect change.*
>
> *Kameen wrote but one more significant article, published in *Boundary 2*, which JB had read. Kameen published in minor, offbeat journals, while JB published in major, organizational journals. And yet, the two read each other and engaged in building on each other. Dialectically.
>
> To anticipate myself, I see Berlin moving from Coleridge's Hegel and dialectics to Marx's and PostMarx's Hegel and dialectics. Also, as we will see, Kameen goes with Heidegger's "languaging" and materialism while JB goes with Marx's 'language materialism.' Heidegger and Marx!?! Some more later.)

To pick up where I last left off, going backwards, I was talking about . . . the third category (audience, new rhetoricians), which is generally described as being **process**-oriented. And had been previously talking about . . . recalling from Kameen's discussion . . . the first two categories (formalism-structuralism and expressivism), which are generally described as being **product**-oriented, given their separation of content from form. Shortly after discussing Coleridge (whom I will return to very soon), Kameen discusses Flower and Hayes as primary process-oriented researchers. And then says Yadda, Yadda, Yadda, which is a scathing critique of their work, which we can go into on another day; for now, I have more important things to get to.

Kameen thereby satisfies the requirement of mapping out the obvious, so that he can now turn to Coleridge and say more explicitly that the poet (who is not a Vitalist!) and his methodology (which he does have!) is neither product-oriented or process-oriented. (Recall that JB had previously drawn the same two conclusions in his "The Rhetoric of Romanticism.")

Let's go back so that we can go forward: For Kameen, D'Angelo gave us the bondage of formal structures imposing on intentionality. Miller and Judy give us no form or structures (anarchy), with the motivation to write arising mysteriously from inner choice. They do not give us, Kameen insists, an alternative to D'Angelo but simply the obverse. Coleridge, however, works not with either self or world, but with **Imagination**, which maintains a dialectical balance between inner/outer, subject/object, self/nature.

Self–>Imagination<–Nature

> Kameen does not make this claim, but I do: If you read these tertiary relationships semiotically in terms of the communications triangle, you will miss them. They are not triangular; they are dialectical. The communications triangle is a map of how communication takes place; a Coleridgean tertiary relationship is a dialectical machine doing and making such things at minimum like the communications map or at maximum like that which has not yet been thought or real-ized.

Kameen further explains:

> As Coleridge suggests, **writing** is neither process nor product, it is both in the continual act of becoming one another; writing is neither self nor world, it is both in the continual act of becoming one another; writing is neither information nor expression, it is both in the continual act of becoming one another. Writing is, most simply, the potential of language being explored under the mutual guidance of writer and reader. (82; emphasis added)

Process–>Writing<–Productwriter–>Language<–Reader

Yes, but what does this all mean? For some insight, we will have to recall the distinction that Kameen makes (and JB had made earlier) between **invention** and **imagination**. (*Which Ann Berthoff has made repeatedly, though not as systematically, as far as I can tell*) Examining what Young and Flower have to say in common about invention (inventing), Kameen points to the metaphor of chase/r, or chasing after a deer in the Baconian woods (85–86). Kameen writes:

> The chase 'of deer in an enclosed park' is an accurate (and devastating) characterization of rigidly formalistic approaches to writing. But let us examine the proposed alternative. While there is no guarantee that the hunter will easily find a deer in the open woods, he does have a very clear idea of what he is searching for, he can make and execute plans to find it, and it is the only thing he *will* find given the goal-directed framework that pre-constitutes his

search. It is on this point that **invention** and **imagination** part company. For the **imagination** is more like an **explorer** than a **chaser**; its mission is not to find a pre-designated something, but to discover the best of what is there to find, to creatively shape that which fills the needs of his 'forethought query.' That may, in fact, be a deer; and it may not.

> Let me stop the flow of this statement by/quotation from Kameen and state that Young's comment, though illustrative of a particular notion of invention (Baconian) is an unfortunate one, and say in parallel fashion, that Kameen's statement, though to the point and illustrative of one aspect of invention, is somewhat unfair in response to Young's views of invention. Why? For the reason that Young's thinking about invention included the idea and possibility of chance, unsearched for, discoveries. Young did not necessarily work out of the Popperian notion of 'Begin with a problem and search for solutions' (P—>S). It is the case, I think, however, that Young in his views on invention had a predilection for starting with a rhetorical problem just as Flower and Hayes had.

This is not to say that the imagination is entirely unfettered by any practical constraints. Far from it, as Coleridge makes clear time and after time. For him imaginative thinking involves purposive (but not goal-directed) forays into the unknown. And such events are guided by the rhetorical relations that maintain among the various aspects of the process—nature, self, and audience—as they intersect in the act of composition. Coleridge's 'method' is designed not only to enhance creative thinking, but also to initiate it.

Invention, therefore, is a fairly mechanical 'special case' of creative thought that **imagination** absorbs into its broader systems. This super-cession is suggested in Coleridge's distinction between the 'secondary imagination' and 'fancy' . . . [*BL* 167] **Imagination** is . . . guided by **method**, and methodological thinking is directed by the will, a kind of induction shaped by constitutive intentionality. **Fancy**, on the other hand, is implemented through choice, the mechanical expression of will when its mission is the routine selection of the most appropriate one from the available many. Will is synthetic: it establishes intentional relations, unifies incommensurable worlds, makes new meanings possible. Choice is integrative: it orders units, selects meanings, assembles groups. In a parallel way, **imagination** shapes wholes, asserts forms, constitutes meanings; **fancy** arranges wholes, discovers forms, constructs meanings. The difference between these two fundamental ways of knowing seems to have been for Coleridge something like that between an **original metaphor** being made and a **dead metaphor** being used. Modern rhetorical theories do, of course, claim that invention can accomplish more than Coleridge provides for fancy. But even if invention is elevated from a subset of imaginative thinking, its function remains relatively mechanical by comparison. (86–87; emphasis added)

Before recalling how Kameen is more explicit about the Imagination being a tertiary process, let's recall his distinction between **process** and **method** in 'endnote 11,' which will take us back to Ron's concern the first night of the seminar about having a methodology and having none. (Ron was responding to Young's chart #1, which is in my Week #1 notes.) Kameen writes:

> The difference between 'process'—as the new rhetoricians use it—and 'method'—as Coleridge uses it—is a significant one. 'Processes' are formal, hierarchical procedures for inquiry; they cannot function without content, but they can be specified and taught as content-independent 'heuristics' that lead to 'solutions' of rhetorical 'problems.' 'Method,' on the other hand, is a dialectical procedure, the shape of which is content-dependent and cannot be precisely prescribed in formal terms; and it is ultimately related to 'truth' as both the motive for and the consequence of effective rhetorical inquiry. In the most general terms, then process models emerge from a philosophical ambience [sic] imbued with Aristotelian and positivistic assumptions about human knowing; method models emerge from a philosophical ambience imbued with Platonic and phenomenological assumptions about human knowing. The former is essentially hierarchical, the latter essentially dialectical. (92)

At the end of his article, Kameen gives us some contemporary examples of people stretching for tertiary processes. Susan Langer and her notion of discursive vs. "non-discursive" ways of communicating and knowing. It is the latter that is like Coleridge's imagination. From Langer, Kameen moves us to Silvano Arieti's *Creativity: The Magic Synthesis*. Arieti works with the notions of **precept** and **concept** but adds an intermediary (tertiary dialectical process) notion of **endocept** (a.k.a. "amorphous cognition"), which blends the two worlds of mind/matter.

Precept–>Endocept<–Concept

This is . . . a Primitive mode of thinking.

Later—let me greatly anticipate myself—Jim will be arguing for the dialectical structure . . . as a primitive form of socialism from P. Freire on. . . .

WRITER→/Utopian Thinking' (Coleridge's Imagination, Rorty's Abnormal Discourse, etc.)→READER

YES, This is, as I am maintaining, a classic Coleridge as proto-Marxist. This is a budding social-epistemic rhetoric. This is socialist rhetoric, or what we will have hope/d it (e/utopically) to become.

JB worked it all out in 1980 though he had not yet made the Marxist connection. It would require many bus rides to work and back with Marx and Marxists in hand. This time on the bus—that JB mentioned to me on many occasions—may have been the most exciting times of his professional reading life.

> **Yet Another Caveat:** Understand that this above commentary about 'Coleridge->Marx' is all my rationalization (secondary revision) after the fact; it's a looking back (a metaleptic turn) to make a different sense of what was to become and now what is. I am not suggesting, therefore, that JB worked consciously or even unconsciously toward this goal of linking Coleridge with Marx. I am suggesting, instead, that there is a good fit between the two, a natural progression from one to the next. A good 'interpretive fit' that will allow us to reread the connection between these two thinkers, Kameen and JB, who shared a similar, though different, experience in the seminar. JB on several occasions made it clear to me that he viewed his development of Kameen's article primarily in terms of refining the epistemological categories, which he did, and of course for political purposes. His refinement is of great importance to the field.

I need to turn now to . . . what I promised in the header: JB's first major article and its impact on theorizing and teaching writing instructions:

JB begins by announcing his disagreement with Fulkerson and others over the importance of "emphasis" on the different elements of the composing process (writer, reality, reader, and language). If you will recall, Fulkerson writes about the confusion among and mindlessness of teachers of composition in relation to what they are teaching. The confusion deals with what Fulkerson calls "modal confusion"; that is, teachers, at the time, were not able to distinguish topologically among the aims of discourse. As a result, in giving assignments, teachers often contradictorily 'emphasized' the expressive aim in giving the assignment but then 'emphasized' the argumentative aim in assessing the assignment. Hence, the confusion. It is the case that Fulkerson is talking about "emphasis" throughout, to which JB responds:

> Pedagogical theories in writing courses are grounded in rhetorical theories, and rhetorical theories do not differ in the simple undue *emphasis* of writer or audience or reality or language or some combination of these. Rhetorical theories differ from each other in the way writer, reality, audience, and language are conceived—both as separate units and in the way the units relate to each other. In the case of distinct pedagogical approaches, these four elements are likewise defined and related so as to describe a different composing process, which is to say a different world with different rules about what can be known, how it can be known, and how it can be communicated. *To teach writing is to argue for a version of reality, and the best way of knowing and communicating it*—to deal, as Paul Kameen has pointed out, in the meta-rhetorical realm of epistemology and linguistics. And all composition teachers are ineluctably operating in this realm, whether or not they consciously choose to do so." (765–66; emphasis added)

And then in direct response to Fulkerson, JB writes:

> The dismay that students display about writing is, I am convinced, at least occasionally the result of teachers unconsciously offering contradictory advice about composing—guidance grounded in assumptions that simply do not square with each other. More important . . . in teaching writing we are tacitly teaching a version of reality and the student's place and mode of operation it it. Yet many teachers (and I suspect most) look upon their vocations as the imparting of a largely mechanical skill, important only because it serves students in getting them through school and in advancing them in their profession. This essay will argue that writing teachers are perforce given a responsibility that far exceeds this merely instrumental task. (766)

Therefore, what JB is attempting to warn teachers and theorists about is the importance of pedagogy in relation to something more than, but which is paradoxically the same as, the teaching of writing, and that is The Teaching of a View or Views of Reality. The teaching of . . . What can be known and not known, understood and not understood, given a particular view of reality! (If the teaching of writing is viewed only as the teaching of consistency in the teaching of the aims, then this is an impoverished view of the teaching of writing!) There is nothing innocent, therefore, about the teaching of literacy! since what is being taught—unbeknownst to most teachers, students, citizens—is not writing per se, but the dominant Reality or, more accurately put, ways of not knowing and not arguing for or against this dominant Reality by way of counter-realitie**s**.

The stakes—political in nature—are the highest. While contrary emphases leading to modal confusion are important to our consideration since such contradictory emphases wreck havoc on *a rhetoric of the classroom*, it must/ought to be understood, in contrast, that a total lack of understanding *how* a particular writing process does exclusively emphasize a particular view of reality is of by far greater importance to our consideration since otherwise such a lack and state of ignorance in the teaching of writing wrecks and will continue to wreck total mindlessness on *a rhetoric of the polis.* And its citizens.

Hence, with litotes, JB writes: ". . . writing teachers are perforce given a responsibility that far exceeds this merely instrumental task" (766). Writing teachers will continue (wittingly or not) to keep students in a subordinate relationship to the dominant discourse—as mere functionaries of this discourse—or will enlighten students of its existence and give them the means of emancipation.

In effect, what JB is attempting is a demystification of an approach to the 'aims' (processes of writing) as formalist and of the teaching of writing just as innocently 'the teaching of writing.' What is implicit in his argument is that writing should be taught as a means of **resisting** the dominant discourse. Which in later articles and books will become

Here's JB's Taxonomy (Epistemic Complex)

The major theme of his work.
- Neo-Aristotelian (or neo-classical)
- Positivist (or Current-Traditional)
- Neo-Platonic (or Expressivist)
- New Rhetoric (or epistemic)

I've often seen people in class stumbling to understand this basic complex—like an infant attempting to become a toddler. It's a rather simple grouping after a while. It's rather elegant. It's powerful heuristically and heretically. It's a continuance of what was read and learned in the NEH seminar but with differences, which I have tried to capture and report above. Dialectically. If any one of you will simply take, say, "reality," and see how each of these dominant modes defines (limits) reality or explores (dialectically) reality/-ies, you will begin to understand the powerful implications of this grouping. Then try semiotical-reading the other elements of the composing process—writer, audience, language—across this complex and see what you come to see.

There is a **logistics**, a **tactic**, and a **strategy** behind the groupings. If these are not understood, then the article with this set of groupings and plot will be—at least, from my perspective—for the most part missed. Not appreciated.

[Note: There's so much to say about Jim's article, but I need to get these notes to you prior to seminar time. I will return and add what wants to be added. -vjv]

—Last updated and corrected: 12 Sept. 1998

Week #4

Notes used for 15 Sept 1998 seminar meeting. –vjv

On The First Book, Writing Instruction, 19th Century, American Colleges |||| With a Special Consideration of the 'The Question Concerning Romanticism':

> Berlin, James A. *Writing Instruction in Nineteenth-Century American Colleges.* Carbondale: SIUP, 1984.

With this book, JB 'begins' his *mature* thinking, by which I mean he is less reliant on the information given him during the NEH Seminar. There is of course a strong residue of that seminar experience. I read his book as a major development and refinement of his previous articles. He is still working with interpreting textbooks (though 18th and 19th century ones), still attempting to determine if a rhetoric is for the social or an individual, still refining and dividing and reframing his basic taxonomy, etc., and employing it tactically and strategically.

His topology now is:
- Classical (from Aristotle and others),
- Psychological-Epistemological (from 18th-century rhetoric),
- Romantic (from the American Transcendental movement).

Dissoi Logoi: Con: These are highly problematic, especially after my 5th reading of the book. When I first read it, I had no major reservations. I think that there are major problems with the description of Emerson as Romantic rhetor. The secular sermonist's/essayist's publishing career is very complex. There are major changes in his attitudes expressed; when he gets to writing "Montaigne; or, the Skeptic" he has a whole new epistemology going for him. It would help anyone to understand Emerson better if s/he would spend some time reading what Emerson's contemporaries had to say, e.g., Melville and taking-into-account powerful biographical forces at work. To read Emerson historically! You cannot freeze Emerson into being a Romantic as JB would render him for his political interests. (I mean you can, but you/JB can only buy trouble for us when you/he forces this rendering, and thereby not following the touted value of 'historicizing' [Jameson] all.) And to read what literary critics also have to say. The split in critical understandings of Emerson by lit critics that JB refers to (Ray vs. Tacey) is a good one to point to, but is selected among others waiting to be selected. Moreover, the attempt to link—for a continuous history, not an "effective history" (Foucault)—Fred Newton Scott as growing out of Emerson, falls really flat. JB himself feels a little uneasy about the connection (see pp. 81–82). Let us also recall that JB sees Scott as having more of a connection with the 19th-century pragmatists (77).

But it's a beginning at a beginning of rethinking the field historically. (There is more to say, but we should wait until the topic of JB and *historiography* comes up.) And therefore . . .

Dissoi Logoi: Pro: JB's position should stand on strategic political terms. I don't want to spend any time here or in class arguing against his casuistic stretching or re-description. But it needs to be understood, as I posted to the listserv for this seminar, that weak arguments for Emerson being a Romantic rhetor different from Coles, etc., and weak arguments for linkages, if bought as successful, can only establish a slippery slope down which the whole edifice of the taxonomies, from Weidner-Young through JB, will go a-tumbling. And everything along with them. Weidner-Young are incorrect, not compelling, but JB(-Kameen) saves them by correcting their readings and by reorganizing the taxonomy. If JB is found no longer compelling, who will rethink the taxonomy, if a taxonomy! To be sure, revision is perpetual.

Let's try another approach for entering the text that is JB's:

Let's begin *in medias* (middle) *res*:

The first two categories (above) are crucial—in my reading of them—in that they lay the groundwork for the previously excluded third (middle), "Romantic," which in extreme forms is the excluded for the sake of civilization, culture, pedagogy, discipline, etc.

CLASSICAL→Romanticism<PSYCHOLOGICAL-EPISTEMOLOGICAL-EPISTEMOLOGIC

> **Reminder:** In seminar last week, I used the notion of "the excluded middle" when discussing Kameen's reading of Coleridge. What I suggested was that in a Platonic-non-platonic, dialectic Kameen is suggesting that Coleridge was establishing a dialectical structure that returned the ever-suppressed excluded middle, and not the Truth. Returned . . . returns us to a "magical synthesis." (Recall the difference between understanding and Reason, or "process" and "method" in endnote #11. Process would give us only identification, the previously known, A=A and possibly A=B (my love = a red, red, rose!), but method would give us the previously unknown, the monstrous, the excluded middle or third, A=Z (in Coleridge's day, love = the woman wailing for her demon lover). Pholks, we are talking about Coleridge here! A strange, uncanny poet!)
>
> Let's remember that Kameen tells us about Arieti who works with the notions of **precept** and **concept** but adds an intermediary (tertiary dialectical process) notion of **endocept** (a.k.a. "amorphous cognition"), which blends the two worlds of mind/matter. Kameen sees this dialectical structure as an extention of Coleridge's dialectical structures.
>
> ---
>
> **Reminder, Uncited references:** JB for some reason or other does not include some important references developed by Ehninger and Scott, in reference to 'systems of rhetoric.' Specifically in relation to Psychological-Epistemological rhetoric. These articles were read by the seminarians and are crucial to an understanding of how JB deals with Campbell and Blair and is establishing and reestablishing topologies of rhetorics in this and later works. The authors, however, speak of "emphases," which JB would not 'think-taxonomies' in this manner and would not agree to. Therefore see:
>
> - Ehninger, Douglas. "On Systems of Rhetoric." *Philosophy and Rhetoric* I (1968):131–44.
> - —. "II: A Synoptic View of Systems of Western Rhetoric." *QJS* 61 (Dec. 1975): 448–53.
> - Scott, Robert. "I. A Synoptic View of Systems of Western Rhetoric." *QJS* 61 (1975): 439–47.
>
> If you were in with me, then you've read these articles and should return to them.

But in rethinking (*in medias res*) these three categories (above), we must heed what JB says in relation to the third, Romanticism. And note that he is concerned with, Which Romanticism? Which Emerson? He writes at the beginning of his chapter 5 on Emerson:

> Several excellent treatments of Emerson's rhetorical thought are available in the literature. These tend to fall into two categories. The first sees Emerson as a romantic individualist, concerned primarily with rhetoric as the expression of the self, without regard for political or social concerns. The second emphasizes Emerson's commitment to democracy—his positioning of the rhetor at the center of political and social action. This position seems to me the more accurate description of Emerson's thought. I will argue that Emerson's rhetoric is preeminently concerned with the role of discourse in the public domain, centering on the place of communication in a modern democracy." (43)

This is an interesting and strategic (species-genus analytics) division that allows JB to enter his discussion about an acceptable Romanticism and Emerson. The political interest and strategy are similar to the ones you will see (have seen) in his article on ideology and composition (*CE*), with expressionism and cognitive psychologism being invited (perhaps unbeknownst to them) to join in on the dialectic. JB baited them and they responded in a colloquy. JB's strategy, then was to call for all parties to speak until they became the party (radically social and democratic) of dialogical exchanges. Dissensus is necessary for social change.

In respect to the topology (above), as JB points out, Aristotelian rhetoric or psychological-epistemological rhetoric (Campbell and Blair) could not deliver the kind of social change he envisioned, which was romantic(-Marxist) and in the best sense of both words.

The issue here is historical, yet Aris/Psychol rhetorics hold on in strange, hybrid forms such as various CTRs (which hold on to bits and pieces of the two categories). But to neutralize these two that still live on in their death, JB has got to introduce and render Romanticism (that which has been excluded in scholarship . . . Weidner-Young, etc.) as he would see it practiced (tho not practiced) in the American College in the 19th century. Let us recall what JB says early in his book:

> Romantic rhetoric places the composing process, the act of writing and speaking, at the center of knowing. Reality is located not in the external world, the realm of the senses and the perceptive faculties, but in the interaction of observer and observed. **A faculty psychology is employed, but it is conceived in completely different dimensions**. . . . (10; bold emphasis added)

In this statement we see illustrated JB's thinking, his revolutionary idea of absorbing and reforming the hostile rhetorics to . . . into a social-epistemic rhetorics.

Yet let us not lose sight and therefore an understanding of the situation that JB is "redescribing" (Rorty): Emerson might have been influential in literature and in our society (self-reliance!) but he was not as influential in the teaching of writing in 19th-century colleges (56). JB states up front that he is dealing with "a close approximation" (56) or a "suspect[ed]" close linkage (56). And as I've said, this will do and for political reasons! Jim's 'method,' as he states up front, is "interpretive" (3).

In speaking of the excluded third/middle, I am not suggesting that JB goes as far as Kameen does in his suggestions. Or as far as I do, and would still go farther down to the rotten, putrified socius. JB never, as far as I know, called for a return of the traditional notion of an excluded middle, say, the *lumpenproletariat*. JB believed that the *lumpenproletariat* (if in a strict sense) would disappear when the economic conditions changed and there was a near-classless society of the *proletariat*.

I am suggesting, once again (as I did last week), that JB is very interested in dialectic by way of Coleridge and that he is laying the groundwork for a Marxist, Post-Marxist dialectic by way of Coleridge/Emerson's Platonic-non-platonic dialectic, or is in parallel fashion constructing a middle term by the common name of '(primitive) e/utopian thinking.' In other words: Later—let me greatly anticipate myself—Jim will be arguing for the dialectical (dialogical) structure . . . as a primitive form of socialism from P. Freire on. . . .

INTERLOCUTOR→/Utopian Thinking' Coleridge's Imagination, Rorth's Abnormal Discourse, etc.)→READER

This, then, is only a suggestion that will be borne out in later discussions. Or not! At best now, it may function as one heuristic suggestion among others for what happens to 'romanticism' when JB's starts establishing and working his way through cultural studies. Therefore, let us not forget the question, What happens to Coleridge, Emerson, Romanticism, in JB's later works on **historiography** and **cultural studies**?

JB writes:

> . . . for Emerson, the ideal can be known only through its manifestation in the external world. At the same time the external world can lead to ideas. The inner and outer have no meaning apart from each other. Truth is a product of a relationship; its source is neither subject nor object, but is located at the point of intersection of the two. Emerson can be seen as anticipating modern epistemology, arguing for reality as the product of the interaction of the perceiver and that which is perceived.
>
> The key to Emerson's epistemology is located in language. Emerson makes the individual the center of the universe, crating meaning through the fusion of idea and matter, of subject and object. The medium of this fusion is language. (47)

Which makes the individual inextricably intertwined in the SOCIAL. But which s.o.c.i.a.l?

Week #5

Notes used for 22 Sept 1998 seminar meeting. —vjv

On The Second Book, *Rhetoric and Reality, Writing Instruction, 20th Century, American Colleges* |||| With a Continued, Special Consideration of the 'The Question Concerning Romanticism':

> Berlin, James A. *Rhetoric and Reality: Writing Instruction in American Colleges, 1900–1985.* Carbondale: SIUP, 1987.

The difference between the first and the second books is immense. While the chapters in the first one in particular are thin, the chapters in the second one are thick with descriptions of information. JB, in his 19th-century book, being one of the first covering that century, had little material to work with; he in his 20th-cenutry book, obviously closer in time and more blessed or cursed with available sources, writes a book that, I think, qualifies as a major 'resource book' itself.

His topology now is:

- Objective Theories,
- Subjective Theories,
- Transactional Theories.

The threesome is more than ever 'Dialectical.' In fact, **I would claim that the whole book is set up in a Hegelian, historical movement toward the Transactional**.

Lest we think that the trio or threefold categories are as simplistic as presented above, we need to attend to the richness of each. Objective Theories in JB's discussions are composed of several subsets or tendencies:

Objective Theories:

- Current-Traditional Rhetoric
- Behaviorist (Robert Zoellner)
- Semanticist (S. I. Hayakawa)
- Linguistic ('Structuralist')

Likewise, Subjective Theories (founded on some philosophy of Idealism) are composed of several tendencies:

- Expressionist (Plato)
- Romanticism/Liberal Culturalist (a particular "strand" of Emerson, Thoreau)
- Depth Psychology (Freud and Post Freudian, C. Rogers and A. Maslow; B. Croce and M. H. Abrams, in literary criticism)

Similarly, Transactional Theories are composed of several tendencies:

- Classical (Baldwin)
- The Cognitive (Emig, Lauer, D'Angelo)
- The Epistemic (from F. N. Scott to Ohmann, Berthoff, Young-Becker-Pike)

Therefore, when I say that the book is dialectical in its structure and its narrative direction, I am suggesting that at the most general level and at its particular levels within each category, the book moves to a historical resolution of social-epistemic. To put a Deleuzian-Guattarian spin on it, I see the expository and argumentative sections becoming-social, almost as much as I see—dialectically—Emerson's *Nature* moving in a similar manner/ism. There is both hope and (I have to emphasize) optimism in this movement.

Let me further refine this statement: The account of histories of the rhetorics of teaching writing do not move, however, in block-like movements toward historical materialist salvation or resolution (the end[s] of history) but move demonstrably yet tentatively, hopefully and optimistically, toward the social. Or better put move as *a perpetual becoming-social*. The struggle is never won, but always waged. What is suggested in this un/kind of movement is that the struggle for making the teaching of writing social requires perpetual vigilance. Perpetual dialogical—poly logical—exchanges among its members.

What Jim has so carefully and strategically done is to pull us into conversation, into rhetorical exchanges about what we do. He situates or locates us in terms of his cognitive re/mappings (Jameson), and asks us, 'Is this where you want to be in relation to these other people attempting the teaching of writing?' And as he puts this question, variously, the question is always an "invocative" (Ede/Lunsford) and provocative question(s).

If Bill Coles tells his students, "I want what you want when you know what you want" (which is only a dangerous half-dialectic in *The Plural I*), JB tells—asks—us, 'Being located here or here, where I situate you in relation to the rest of us, Is this what you want for US?' It's a very forceful, not-easy-to-deflect tactical question . . . that JB puts to each of us.

Such a question put to you or me—to us—requires that we respond. Which we do.

And thereby, JB perpetually reestablishes the conditions for further possible social-epistemic exchanges. (JB studied Invention from Richard Young in the NEH seminar, studied the various processes and methodologies, but himself became an interventional machine. This is his ethos: Becoming-Interventional.) Linda Flower read JB, was invoked and provoked, responded to JB, and became social . . . for us and most importantly in her research and publications for US and our mutual students.

> I find this wonderfully ironic in its collaborative structure: JB made two protocols for Flower/Hayes, became an Object, a rat running the composition maze for them. Then, later, he wrote about, ever so indirectly himself and the rest of us as Objects, liberating us all from the research-cum-pedagogical protocol produced by Flower/Hayes. . . . Which eventually and finally liberated Flower.
>
> Let's call it, as Baudrillard would, 'the revenge of the Object.'

Yes, I realize that I am stretching all this, drawing a cause-effect relationship here, but it's only what I can do in an attempt to describe my readings of JB's book. And others' readings. Our readings. In a rather 'collaborative' world, what we read, think, write, say, teach, learn has an effect on all of us. If seeing an object affects that object in toto, teaching a student how to write or think about writing affects all of us. Invoking colleagues, provoking them, bending and stretching a reading toward the social, cannot but bring about change. Socially and Epistemically. These are—as I would hopefully and optimistically think—ethical and political becoming-readings. Yes, it is becoming-of-us to re/think perpetually in this—if so, ill—mannered (baroque) way.

JB writes:

> Rhetoric . . . becomes implicated in all human behavior. All truths arise out of dialectic, out of the interaction of individuals within discourse communities. Truth is never simply "out there" in the material world or the social realm, or simply "in here" in a private and personal world. It emerges only as the three—the material, the social, and the personal—interact, and the agent of mediation is language. (17)

Right after this statement, JB goes on to respond to Bob Connors's review of his 19th-century history. I will take up this response when we discuss JB and historiography.

End of notes this time around: But here's a question that I want you to ponder for this evening's seminar: How does JB, in this discussion of 20th-century writing instruction in the U. S., return to his discussions of Emerson (Thoreau), Dewey, and F. N. Scott? Or to his discussions of "Brahminical romanticism" or "mandarin romanticism"? And how are these various personages or literary categories now connected? in the unfolding narrative? And what were your thoughts as JB reintroduces Macrorie, Murray, Coles, and Elbow? (pp. 151–55).

Did you see the reference to Dewey and Hegel on p. 59? Interesting!?

How and what is the significance of JB's dealing with the ever-shifting dialectic of rhetoric-poetics?

What parallels do you see between or among the unfolding history of the actual teaching of writing, the development of departments of English (literature in the vernacular, the inclusion of American Literature and the teaching of Writing/Rhetoric), and the apparently unplanned institution of professional organizations (MLA, NCTE, CCCC)?

More serendipitous questions to come!

Week #6

Notes Used for 29 Sept 1998 Seminar Meeting. –vjv

Historiography I, |||| With a Continued, Special Consideration of Dialectic/s

Now we are taking up the issue of historiography, that is, the rhetoric/s of history writing. The movement from what we have been discussing to this new topic should be an easy transition. And a counter-logical one. By which I mean: (1.) We act, write, speak, etc. and then, we give an explanation of how (rationalization, secondary revision) we performed the deed. I say 'counter-logical' to the process of writing history because there is the notion that we (should) begin with a principle of historiography first and then we begin writing our histories. This is seldom, if ever the case, at least in rhetoric or in composition studies, up to 1987. (If there is an exception to this experiential rule, I guess I would have to point to Robert Connors, who did deliver and publish a work on historiography prior to JB's first article or prior to "the historiography group's" publishing anything. ('Historiography Group' = Susan Jarratt, John Schilb, JB, and VV, who published twice, as a group, yet separately, on historiographies in PRE/TEXT.)

> *Historiography and the Histories of Rhetorics I: Revisionary Histories* and *Historiography and the Histories of Rhetorics II: Revisionary Histories and Ethics* in PRE/TEXT (Spring/Summer 1987) and (Fall/Winter 1990).

I think that all this sequencing of events vis-a-vis the writing-of-history process needs further clarification, hence (2.): In general, the field of composition considers writing as basically 'metaleptic,' which means that the thesis, story, etc. or the question or problem arises out of the answering or solving of each. What JB and the Historiography Group attempted—and somewhat in keeping with the notions of a metaleptic composing process—was to say, in a counter-logical way that the writer of histories of rhetoric and/or composition **should know**, prior to writing, what his or her particular historiographical procedure or ideology would be. If you recall, JB at the beginning of the first two books spells out his biases, his historiographical principles (not objective, but politically interested, social-epistemic). Recall JB's response in *Rhetoric and Reality* to Bob Connors's attack on his first book. Jim writes:

> His [BC's] assumptions here and in much of his own historical research is that it is possible to locate a neutral space, a position from which one can act as an unbiased observer in order to record a transcendental object, the historical thing-in-itself. Those who write history from this vantage point, he claims, are objective and scholarly, providing research especially developed for specialists, research which is, at its best, definitive—meaning, presumably, that its authoritativeness brings discussion to a close. Those who do not share this neutral vantage point are subjective and biased, have 'an axe to grind,' and offer what is, at most, 'popular history.'" (17). JB's says all this after he has spelled out his historiographical principles, not just to report the so-called "facts" but to report them, as he cannot but, as "interpretations. (As Nietzsche says: facts = interpretations.)

Still more clarification here: (3.): First comes the historiographical principles, or set of biases; that is, first comes the acknowledgement of biases and what they are, and then comes the writing of the history, and then comes the question or problem arising out of the answering or solving of each. All in a social exchange arises out of language. Hence:

Historiographical →Composing ✷The Question or Problem
Historiographical →Composing →The Question or Problem.

To understand fully this flowing direction, however, it is necessary to be aware that the initial historiographical principles themselves can change, and often do:

HP -> Composing ->The Q or P –> New Historiographical Principles

An Aside: Often you will hear from historians in rhetoric/composition that some people write history while others only write about writing history. This is a very interesting Platonic argument! against historiography. I would hope and pray (if necessary, prey) that this incipient and insipid argument, value judgment, can be seen for what it is.

> Berlin, James A. "Revisionary History: The Dialectical Method." *PRE/TEXT* 8.1–2 (1987): 47–61.

I want to move on now—with this intro out of the way, or in the way—to JB's article. I think, believe, it's important to keep in mind that when JB wrote this first article he was writing it with the knowledge that three other people were writing an article on and for the same issue. There was, during the writing, talk and questions such as "Are you using so-and-so, etc." There was, in my recollection, a certain amount of apprehension, since so little . . . really nothing . . . had been done on historiography in the field, and that consequently many people would be reading the articles. Or at least glancing at them.

In retrospect—what else is there?—I am going to intrude and give *my "reading"* of what JB is at least incipiently doing in this first article: Note that immediately he divides his task (as all great dialecticians do): "In arriving at revised versions of the history of rhetoric, two projects must be attempted: a critique of the histories that have so far been written and a theoretical description of the histories that ought to follow" (48). What I casuistically take this to mean, that is, what I stretch this opening statement to mean, is a dialectical past-future, or what I eventually would and did call the "future perfect" or "future-anterior."

> See Victor J. Vitanza, "Taking A-Count of a (Future-Anterior History of Rhetoric as Libidinalized Marxism (A PM Pastiche)." In *Writing History of Rhetoric*. Vitanza. SIUP.

In this approach there would be a shuttling or dialogical exchange between the **past** and the **future** to produce new histories in the **present**. The historian would thereby move us/the field from failed past to e/utopian future in order to locate but produce a *provisionary* history in the present.

What JB says in this article is in great part a repetition of what he has said historiographically in his first two books. But—and this is important—JB takes on [*sic*., double articulation intended] Foucault here. He tells us that his discussion of the past is to be in terms of "the first part of" (48) Foucault's discussions in "Nietzsche, Genealogy, History" [*Language, Counter-Memory, Practice*. Ed. Donald F. Bouchard. Ithaca: Cornell UP, 1977.].

Only the first part! What he will take is Foucault's gift of Power and Knowledge as "indistinguishable," and Knowledge as "rhetorical" (48). What he will reject, take on (argue against and exclude) is everything else, especially, what JB sees as a form of determinism in Foucault. **For JB, History is Human**, for the most part. JB sided with Marx, not a Focaultean Post-Marx.

Let us recall: As Marx says: "Men make their own history, but they do not make it just as they please; they do not make it under circumstances chosen by themselves, but under circumstances directly encountered, given and transmitted from the past" (See Marx, *Eighteenth Brumaire*... NY: International Publishers, 1984: 15.) This, indeed, is a complicated statement, but JB took it to mean, emphasizing the optimistic part, that we set in motion history and that we can make adjustments in its directions, when things go wrong, as Marx himself believed in his Humanistic writing. The attempts at adjustments, of course, are not always successful. I, however, read the statement in the larger overall context of the book in "joyfully pessimistic" terms (Nietzsche *The Birth of Tragedy*; Foucault). I don't want to get into this in detail here, for I have a lengthy article forthcoming very soon in the British cultural studies journal *Parallax* on this very subject, an article dis/entitled "The Hermeneutics of Abandonment." What I do want to get into here, however, is JB's rejection of Foucault's full position. It is crucial to understand the ideological difference that exists between JB and Foucault when it comes to history writing. And though I will not take them up at this point in the seminar or spend that much time on them, but will wait until the end at the appropriately scheduled time for stating such differences, the DIFFERENCES are immensely expensive, I believe, in the long run of history.

What does JB reject and exclude from Foucault in writing a historiographical principle? He writes:

> The flaw in his position is that it also contains contradictory anti-rhetorical elements. For Foucault the particular power-knowledge relationship (...genealogy) that marks a given historical period forms an all but seamless web of constraints, enclosing all acts in an invisible and inescapable net. All reality—both subject and object—is constructed by these power-knowledge relations and there is virtually no evading them. Change, within these formations, furthermore, is not only unpredictable but cannot be accounted for, being caused by an irrational eruption. This is why Foucault emphasizes the necessity of history assuming 'the form of a concerted carnival' (161), a celebration of diversity and deviance, the joy of the unexpected and comic. Resistance is, to be sure, inevitable and is to be encouraged, even though it may end only in serving the forces resisted. The problem with Foucault's notion of resistance, as pointed out by Dreyfus and Rabinow in a volume sympathetic to his thought, is that it provides no standards on which to resist. (50–51)

Meant im/possibly for Jim: Yes, history writing, critiquing, and predicting is not a science. If I were completely and exclusively a Marxian Humanist, I indeed would be turned off by, or disappointed with, Foucault's notion of history. "Effective History." With its cut-ups and chance occurrences. But

I am also a Marxian Non-Humanist in terms of Marx's writings in *The German Ideology*: ". . .circumstances make men just as much as men make circumstances" (165; in *The Marx-Engels Reader*. 2nd Ed. Edited by Robert C. Tucker. NY: Norton, 1978). I accept the contradiction that is Marx. The contra-Diction/Para-Dox that he himself accepts as himself. I accept all that is the excluded middle! I accept the Hermaphrodite Marx, as Lyotard depicts him/her/it in *Libidinal Economy*: "The old Man [Marx] is also a young woman to us, a strange bisexual assemblage" (96). The new duplicity! A *hermaphrodite*. The imminent reversal of the sign, no longer anchored, but theatrically drifting. What Lyotard notices in the (hoaxful, duplicitous, on its way to becoming triplicitous) text, and invites us to notice, is that "The old Man" of the text is dis/engaged in perpetual invention; is dis/engaged in "the perpetual postponement of finishing work on *Capital*, a chapter becoming a book, a section a chapter, a paragraph a section, by a process of cancerization of theoretical discourse, by a totally pulsional proliferation of a network of concepts hitherto destined on the contrary to 'finalize,' to 'define' and to justify a proletarian politics" (96–97). I accept the complexity and the contradictions in and among the many voices—in the Mad Text—of Marx. To say that we are to accept only the rational Marx and not the non-rational or irrational Marx is problematic for me: I cannot but accept what is fully, complexly Human in Marx! Human Beings are not the rational measures of all things. There is more than one (libidinal) economy at work and play here and there. In rhetorics and poetics.

Meant possibly for the seminarians: I have said and argued (above, still as pre-amble, ambling) that there is an incipient dialectic between **past and future to produce a provisional present**. I think and believe that this is the fuller promise of what JB is aiming for, wittingly or unwittingly. Such an incipient dialectic must have a view of the SOCIAL that does not exclude in order to have what goes for a 'socially-acceptable' social. I believe that this is what wants to be said, or overheard and then said, in terms of JB's article.

If there is this incipient dialectic in JB's article, I must ask and attempt to answer and pay attention to the explicit dialectic in his article. I must represent what needs to be said. Let us in that dispirited way, then, return to the initial division and, then leaping to the next page for time referents—which were previously in my reading past and future with a middle present (with all a Deleuzian Socius), but which are in JB's self-reading past and present with a middle attenuated social—read what JB says:

Again, JB distinguishes "previous histories" from "the new histories." Previous historians have assumed "that there are moments of time in which the essential features of the one true rhetoric can be directly observed. For the classisist, this moment is in the past, in the rhetoric of ancient Greece or Rome" (49). And "for the modern . . . the essence of rhetoric is to be found in the here and now, at the end of a long succession of historical progress" (49).

PAST←--" (Previous Historians II --→ "PRESENT" (Modern Historians)

What would be new in the writings of the histories of written communication—beyond the classicist and modernist—is "to see the formal statements of this discipline [of written communication] as a study that is at the center of social activity" (52). Again, Berlin interjects the topos of the social (or dialectics) as the ground for revision. The dialectical method that is to be employed on "the center" is a rhetoric, or rhetorics, that would mediate between the "material and social conditions of society" and "the political and cultural" conditions (52). To give us a new Future (history).

"Material and Social Conditions of Society" ←The Social→ "The Political and Cultural" Conditions

Berlin explains:

> The ability to read, write, and speak in accordance with the code sanctioned by a culture's ruling class is the main work of education, and this is true whether we are discussing ancient Athens or modern Detroit. These rules are of course inscribed in a rhetoric, a systematic designation of who can speak, when and where they can speak, and how they can and must speak. Educational institutions inculcate these rules, determining who is fit to learn them and who has finally done so—in other words, who is authorized to be heard. A rhetoric codifies these rules for the members of a society. It is therefore never simply a set of disembodied principles that discuss the way language is used for purposes of persuasion or communication. It is a set of strictures regarding the way language is used in the service of power. It designates who may have access to power and who may not, doing so in a way even more effective than legal sanctions with all of their punitive devices. To use Althusser's terms a rhetoric serves as an important ideological state apparatus. It affirms economic, social, political, and cultural arrangements, doing so in the name of passing on to the young the 'natural' rules that govern discursive and, more important, non-discursive practices. (52)

Berlin would, therefore, have us study dialectically the ideological structures called *how to speak, how to write*, and in general, *how to communicate*, which are used to determine the business of the polis. We must also study dialectically, however, the oppositional, discounted ideological ways to produce a revolutionary discourse that, Berlin says, calls "into question the social and political formulations of its rivals" (54). He reminds us, "There are always competing rhetorics at any historical moment because there are always competing ideologies, and this is demonstrable despite the fact that our rhetorical histories have attempted to ignore this conflict" (54–55). At this moment, Berlin draws a bridge between writing and having these histories and using them in education: *It is the cultural, ideological conflicts that are to be taught in the schools*. Hence, Berlin would want us to employ a plurality of approaches, but always for ethico-political purposes (56–58). He would have us rebegin a revision of history by understanding that "our only hope in not being able to know everything . . . is to know as many versions of the whole as we can, as many conceptual systems in their concrete application as possible" (59).

The many versions and conceptual systems are precisely what Berlin locates in his taxonomies of 19th- and 20th-century histories of writing instruction. Would he claim that his taxonomies are *the* taxonomies? Of course, not! He would, instead, have us locate yet other versions and systems and to bring them into conflict with his. This exchange, then, would be the realization of the dialectical principle at work, with the hope of including minoritarian voices into the discussion.

> Berlin, James A. "Postmodernism, Politics, and the Histories of Rhetoric." *PRE/TEXT* 11.3–4 (1990): 169–87.

As we turn, and we must turn, to the second article, we see a continuation of less the species problem (i.e., Foucault) but the generic problem (i.e., the Postmodern). Which will lead again back to the idea of a provisional grand narrative of emancipation. But Note how JB begins by distancing himself from the p/t issue-topic of ethics: He is well aware that the focus of ethics is on the individual and, therefore, he must maneuver back to the social (170). He then continues by surveying what is problematic for him in dis/respect to Postmodernism: namely, the non-status of the subject, the shunning of totalizing (grand) narratives, and the priority of signifying practices (171). He points out in passing how historians do, in fact, hold on to the idea of getting at reality unmediated, which Pomo and Marxism dispel as possible. But he then turns to Paul Smith (*Discerning the Subject*) in order to take up the problematics of Pomo, specifically, in respect to the problem of the ethical subject. JB—as I myselves—find in Smith a subject that is multiple, but in terms of a dialectic of complex subject-social formations, not as a schizo-subject that would only reject and outwit Kapital. The latter of which is a different story. JB finds in this subject position an interaction among the various subjects within a subject that does not give priority to the signifying practice, as is generally found in Pomo. And then and most importantly—to the very last, posthumous publication of his final book—JB sets aside grand narratives and little narratives in favor of what is called 'provisional [grand] narratives.' (The move is analogically similar to Marxist critics setting aside naive essence for 'strategic essence'

(Spivak) so as to establish some kind of provisional subject-agent.) This is simply a making of philosophical narrative into a rhetorical, perhaps sophistic, narrative. (I think that this is a very dangerous move but I will return to critique it later at the appropriate point in the seminar.) JB writes:

> I would propose the necessity for provisional, contingent narratives in attempting to account for the past and present. While history may be marked by no inherent plan or progression, it is the product of complex interactions of people, social institutions, ideologies, technological conditions, and modes of production. To abandon the attempt to make sense of history is to risk being victimized by it.

JB now becomes rather interesting and goes back and picks up his early NEH seminar in Invention:

He rebegins to talk about this provisional grand narrative in interventional terms, that is, as a heuristic:

> Contingent narratives then become heuristics that open up 'mediations, interrelations, and interdependencies that give shape and power to larger political and social systems' (70, quoting Aronowitz and Giroux, *Postmodern Education*). To use Jameson's formulation, such narratives provide cognitive maps which at the simplest level are indispensable to daily experience, providing 'that mental map of the social and global totality we all carry around in our heads in variously garbled forms' (415). For projects as complex as the writing of history, complex cognitive maps that serve as provisional heuristic devices for responding to the vast array of data are indispensable. Indeed, in a remarkable departure from Marxist tradition, Jameson even places the concept of the base/superstructure relationship in this category, identifying it as 'a starting point and a problem, an imperative to make connections, as undogmatic as a heuristic recommendation simultaneously to group culture (and theory) in and for itself, but also in relation to its outside, its content, its context, and its space of intervention and effectivity' (*Postmodern* 409). The guiding narratives to be invoked in writing history here recommended similarly offer this capacity to provide connections while near determining in advance exactly what they will be. The narrative and the facts it discovers engage in a dialectical interaction in which the two terms of the encounter are always open to revision, the narrative revealing data while the data revises the narrative. (176–77)

Several pages later (beginning, 180), JB takes up the interventional procedure in terms of "heuristics of historiography." But specifically in terms of the communications triangle: writer, reader, language, reality. He demonstrates, as Hayden White would (*Tropics of Discourse*), that particular rhetorical theorists (Aristotle, Campbell, etc.) are produced—invented—by particular epistemologies/signifying practices. **Caution:** These theorists are not determined by these practices, but can be revised as subjects just as our interpretations of them can be revised. Thereafter, unto the end of the article, JB falls into 'the systems of rhetoric game' previously practiced by Ehninger and Scott and by himself. JB . . . looks like a formalists, demonstrating how signifying practices *produce* different views of Plato, etc.

Recall what JB wrote: Against Foucault: "Change, within these formations, furthermore, is not only unpredictable but cannot be accounted for, being caused by an irrational eruption. This is why Foucault emphasizes the necessity of history assuming 'the form of a concerted carnival'" (161). What JB has done, it bears repeating, is to make *change* accountable in terms of a formalist, interventional procedure, just as White (*Tropics*) had.

Having accomplished this somewhat moment of predictability, JB leaves behind, deflects, the issue of chance. He, like White, says "No" to the absurdist moment in history writing. The repressed, however, forever returns. It is irrepressible no matter what single geometry is placed on it to filter it out, to numb it, to quiet it. (To the point that he does not even make the somewhat acceptable purring of the beast. At rest and with contentment.) Down. For . . . If only a while.

To re/capitulate: We might say that JB's provisional or contingent [grand] narrative can alter our views of all that is in THE history of rhetoric so that we can practice a ethico-political revisions of THE history remaking them into competing histories.

Thus, we can use his view of writing histories of rhetoric for, at least, until the repressed irrational/ity of the beast, the other unfettered desire, returns.

There is so much here that I want to intervene into to, but again appropriate time will have come.

Octalog, The Octalog, I have provided as a context, a socially demonstrable dialectic at work. I can only now say—with time running short before the Seminar—that it was an occasion, a rare occasion. So rare that it has proved to be, so far, unique and therefore irrational and non-repeatable. It's as if it all never happened. Never made an iota of difference. The history of rhetoric remains as oppressive as it ever has been.

An Incomplete, Highly-Selected Chronology of Recent Works Specifically on Historiography of Rhetoric:

1979: James J. Murphy, "The A-Historians Guide: Or, Ten Negative Commandments for the Historian of Rhetoric" In *H Texnh: Proceedings of the Speech Communication Association Doctoral Honors Seminar*. Ed. Richard Enos and William E. Wiethoff. n.p.

1984: Robert Connors, "Historical Inquiry into Composition Studies." *The Writing Instructor* 4 (Summer): 157–67.

1987: PRE/TEXT Special Interest Group Panel, Revisionary Histories, at College Composition and Communication Conference, Atlanta, March. The panel included James Berlin, Bill Covino, Susan Jarratt, Jan Swearingen, Victor Vitanza.

1987: Victor J. Vitanza, "Critical Sub/Versions of the History of Philosophical Rhetoric." *Rhetoric Review* 6.1 (Fall): 41–66.

1987: William Covino, *The Art of Wondering: A Revisionist Return to the History of Rhetoric*. Boynton/Cook.

1987: *Historiography and the Histories of Rhetorics I: Revisionary Histories. PRE/TEXT* (Spring/Summer): articles by Susan Jarratt, John Schilb, James A. Berlin, Victor J. Vitanza.

1988: Writing Histories of Rhetoric Conference, Arlington TX.

1988: Octalog. "The Politics of Historiography." (1988 CCCC Panel): Jerry Murphy, James Berlin, Robert Connors, Sharon Crowley, Victor Vitanza, Susan Jarratt, Nan Johnson, Jan Swearingen. *Rhetoric Review* 7.1 (Fall): 5–49.

1988: George Kennedy, "Some Reflections of Neo-Modernism"; Robert Scott, "Non-Discipline as a Remedy for Rhetoric? A Reply to Victor Vitanza"; Michael Leff, "Serious Comedy: The Strange Case of Dr. Vitanza." *Rhetoric Review* 6.2 (Spring): 230–45.

1990: *Historiography and the Histories of Rhetorics II: Revisionary Histories and Ethics. PRE/TEXT* (Fall/Winter): articles by Susan Jarratt, John Schilb, James A. Berlin, Victor J. Vitanza.

1993: Takis Poulakos, Ed. *Rethinking the History of Rhetoric*. Boulder: Westview P.

1994: Victor J. Vitanza, Ed. *Writing Histories of Rhetoric*. Carbondale: SIUP.

Week #7

Notes Used for 6 Oct. 1998 Seminar Meeting. –vjv

Ideology, |||| With a Continued, Special Consideration of Dialectic/s

> Berlin, James A. "Rhetoric and Ideology in the Writing Class." *College English* 50.5 (Sept. 1988): 477–94.

Now we are taking up the issue of ideology, that is, the relation between ideology and rhetoric. This "that is" is important! For it defines Rhetoric as not above Ideology, in a hierarchical relationship, but within Ideology, subject to it, but not necessarily subjected to it.

Desired interruptions, PROLOGUEs: The meaningS of Ideology are difficult to understand, to follow, for the path is not clear. Ideology itself is plural, without any one definition serving as arbiter over competing definitions. While Rhetoric cannot serve as an arbiter of Ideologies, Ideologies cannot themselves serve as an arbiter of Rhetorics. Or can Ideologies do the latter? More specifically, Can **Social-epistemic ideology** serve as arbiter? JB would have it as such. Given the alternatives (cogs and expressionists)—rounded up and put on display as the usual suspects—I would agree.

This is a question that we would desire—f/or desire would have us?—to answer: "Yes, I would agree," he volunteers so quickly! Ideology/ies would drive our desires to know the answer to this question. . . . "I" am compelled. And yet, my/our desire finally would not let me/us, if at all possible, know that we are driven. But would let us, nonetheless, have our way with the answer. Marx is quite good on this subject: "They do this without being aware of it" (*Capital I*, 166–67). But in being aware of "it," would we be any better off? Could-cum-Would this awareness be good and possible?

Let me begin on a(nother) wrong foot. And ask these questions while-reading (a wild, savage-reading of) JB's by now canonized article "Rhetoric and Ideology in the Writing Class":

"That is" is that which exists. ("That is" is not epiphenomenal, but phenomenal, i.e., material.) But where does "That is" exist? except in ideology? Where does a clear enough (i.e., ethical, aesthetic) understanding of Ideology exist? (Yes, I am conflating what exists and what is good.) The answer of course to this question "Where?" is in the *conditions* of social transactions. (For Freire, it would be in the very *conditions of the logos:*"If men are searchers and their ontological vocation is humanization, sooner or later they may perceive the contradiction in which banking education seeks to maintain them, and then engage themselves in the struggle for their liberation" [*Pedagogy of the Oppressed* 61–62]. Ontological vocation = Being-to-freedom calling us to ourselves and then to itself.)

Why is the "clear enough" good? Is not clarity the most metaphysical, Ideal of concepts? (Marx is so elegantly clear.)

> Žižek, Slavoj. *The Sublime Object of Ideology* NY: Verso, 1989.

I remember R. Young saying, "Marx's prose is the clearest." Which it is! Therefore, is Marx's clear enough definition "enough"? What then of Freire's? Therborn's? And as far as Marx goes, What then of Žižek's questioning of Marx's definition? Are Žižek's permutations and further complications even enough?) How many different perspectives on "What is ideology?" would we need to have enough "clear enough" answers? KB writes: "By adding one more confusion, we may add the element that can bring clarity" (*RM*, 10)

Forget the question(s)! Let me/us further problematize what I am desiring as a question: **Be(a)ware:** The Ideology of Clarity is NOT the subject of my desire, nor the desire of my subject, here! If not, then what?

These two—that is, exist(ence) and good—are important. No doubt! But the third and its corollary fourth (question) are overwhelmingly important, casting more light, yet darkness, and then the inevitable grayness (?!) on their asking:

Not "Where is it?," But

> **How is it?,**
>
> **how is it good?,**
>
> **and how is it possible?**
>
> Or

> How is it for me/us?
>
> How is it good for me/us?
>
> and How is it possible for me/us?
>
> When the "That is" comes from the conditions of the Impossible?

Beings thrown into this condition can but make for sado masochism.

These questions—my questions of doubt, doubtful questions—exist as not good, beautiful, but ugly, monstrous, even sublime: The word is "Conditions": the conditions of the *logos* (language, reasoning), the conditions of material existence. What we are wrestling with here (angel or devil or still a more terrible monster yet to be included into the social-epistemic exchange) is Definitions. The "What is?" syndrome. Ontological definitions. (We cannot say accurately that JB was not concerned with Ontology, but only Epistemology! The two are inextricably intertwined. Recall Freire above, his ontological vocation as the condition for being called to freedom and knowing, recognizing, freedom.) . . . Questions as Definitions. What exists? Whether it is Good, Whether it is Possible. . . .

Am I about to dis/engage in a deconstructive act here on these Questions? On Berlin's article on Ideology that would use these questions? From Therborn? Perhaps! Again Recall, as Gayatri Spivak is prone to recalling from Derrida on many occasions: "deconstruction has always been about the limits of epistemology" ("feminism and deconstruction, again" 209).

And Recall, as Spivak is equally given to recalling from Heidegger: "*Dasein* is ontically programmed to ask the ontological question, *and* not to be able to answer it. This is undoubtedly a corrective for any account [logos] which assumes that when we work for an epistemological itinerary [social-epistemic?] to cleanse the ontological account [logos, narrative] of ourselves, this might contribute or, indeed, lead to correct psycho-sexual [or any other] political action" (209).

I do not ReCall up these specters from the past to neutralize JB's position vis-a-vis the ideology of social-epistemic rhetorics. Even if I were, neutralization could and would never occur. Corrections, if not Deflections, of my corrections are inevitable, if from no one but my-selves. And perhaps this might be the social-epistemic encounter or moment itself! But I think not. For I am deeply and superficially concerned with the Conditions that bring all this into *being* and *knowing*.

Definitions/Questions are founded on the conditions of the Negative. Definition is the Limit(ing condition-cum-heuristic) of understanding. Definition (Aristotelian, species + genus + differentiae) is a byproduct of dialectic, which is a byproduct—yet ever a commodity to be sold, bartered for—

bye way of The Negative. More simply put, we say what something is bye way of saying what it is not. As the cliche by now goes, presence is absence; absence is presence, yada, yada, yada.

How then is existence and the good made politically-socially acceptable WHEN from the Symbolic, the Negative, WHEN from a goodness (desire) called Lack? **In this dire situation—in this locating Negative, this negating Location—The Truth, as we nostalgically hungered and still hunger for it, is no longer possible; it is impossible; therefore, all is possible, but must be arbitrated via a social-perpetual dialectic, which in turn may prove to be impossible. The snake eating its tail; the tale eating its snake.** (Therborn, Aristotle, and Gorgias, given the negative, are but the same semiotically stretched across the Negative!) This good and possible world view, however, is . . . rather can be . . . an existential good. We have agreed on that. Provisionally. But. . . .

These questions—my questions of doubt, doubtful questions—exist as not good, but ugly, monstrous. Stupid! Stupid! Stupid! Therefore, they do not exist, nor are they good, nor can they ever give us the possible as an acceptable policy for life's brutish shortcomings.

> I am not so subtly suggesting here that Therborn's "What exists? What is good? What is possible?" are parallel with the ancient threefold propositions of Fact, of Value, and of Policy.

But Why ugly, monstrous? These questions 'originate' in the possible that is not linked with the impossible. Are not linked with or determined by the conditions of the Symbolic. The Negative. Consequently: They originate outside of—or originate as a remainder of—the conditions for the possibilities of Ideology/ies themselves. Outside species-genus analytics. Outside the Ideology of ideologies. Outside of any human concern for What is? and What is a/the good? and What is clear about existence and a/the good? Outside of any concern for saving the Polis for a select few or apparently for all. But inside the concerns of the "Inhuman." (I am not speaking of the In humane!, which is the Human trying to be more Human, creating remainders [ex nihilo], excluding all other things as being Not Human, excluding bye way of the principles of Identification, of non-contradiction, and of excluded middle.)

Is there an alternative to the possible that is the impossible, an escape from the desire that is called (ontologically called, epistemologically called) from Lack? And therefore can but take us to a Hell in our search for perfection. Saving the world and its content by killing it? Save us for our desire for power (individual or social), for a "fascism," as Foucault says, "in us all, in our heads and in our everyday behavior, the fascism that causes us to love power, to desire the very thing that dominates and exploits us" (Preface to *Anti-Oedipus*, xiii). Yes the power to overthrow power. Power to the People! Power to the Human. To Become-more-human. Than Human. The fascism that would cause me to write, in response, this very 'correction' to my reading of JB's "Rhetoric and Ideology in the Writing Class"!

Lyotard, who is no longer human, if he ever was, writes:

> . . . education. If humans are born human, as cats are born cats (within a few hours), it would not be . . . I don't even say desirable, which is another question, but simply possible, to educate them. That children have to be educated is a circumstance which only proceeds from the fact that they are not completely led by nature, not programmed. The institutions which constitute culture supplement this native lack.
>
> What shall we call human in humans, the initial misery of their childhood, or their capacity to acquire a 'second' nature which, thanks to language, makes them fit to share in communal life, adult consciousness and reason? That the second depends on and presupposes the first is agreed by everyone. The question is only that of knowing whether this dialectic, whatever name we grace it with, leaves no remainder.
>
> If this were the case, it would be inexplicable for the adult himself or herself not only that s/he has to struggle constantly to assure his or her conformity to institutions and even to arrange them with a view to a better living-together, but that the power of criticizing them, the pain of supporting them and the temptation to escape them persist in some of his or her activities. I do not mean only symptoms and particular deviancies, but what, in our civilization at least, passes as institutional: literature, the arts, philosophy. There too, it is a matter of traces of an indetermination, a childhood, persisting up to the age of adulthood." (*The Inhuman* 3)

Some interesting thoughts on a whole shitload of what I/we have heretofore said (above). And yet, Does it not sound . . . like an Expressivist point of view well within, yet not at all within, but from outside the Social-Epistemic? Does it not sound like a 'remainder'? And do not the words, once again, raise the specter of the rhetorics-poetics split Wild counter-raising their togetherness, their inextricable togetherness? Do not the words sound as if coming from the Inhuman itself?

Maybe: A(nother) question to guide us through, down, and eventually—it is hoped (desired)—away from this path, that has served as the fecundity of all thinking, this path of the Negative:

What would existence, the good, and the possible, What could Thinking become if not originating from the Symbolic, the negative . . . the IMPOSSIBLE? Itselfs? What would Inhuman thinking be (become) and how would it be known as . . . simply as. A place, as Lyotard would have it, a *Pagus*, not a Polis, where "the monstrous and the formless have their rights because they can be sublime" (97).

The lumpenproletariat will never disappear by simply fixing an immoral economy that, Marx thought and JB agreed with, produces them. There is a very different economy, libidinal-materialist economy, at play here, that would accept, reinclude the heretofore remainders, left, far left over from being excluded at the middles/muddles.

If we are proceeding dialectically, we are proceeding—in a non-progressive way—toward the Inhuman.

I am a Berliner, but I am also (contradictorily) a Victorine, a member of that heretical aesthetic sect during the Middle Ages.

But let's attend to Rhetoric and Ideology:

JB writes:

> Instead of rhetoric acting as the transcendental recorder or arbiter of competing ideological claims, rhetoric is regarded as always already ideological. This position means that any examination of a rhetoric must first consider the ways its very discursive structure can be read so as to favor one version of economic, social, and political arrangements over other versions. A rhetoric then considers competing claims in these three realms from an ideological perspective made possible both by its constitution and by its application—the dialectical interaction between the rhetoric as text and the interpretive practices brought to it. A rhetoric can never be innocent, can never be a disinterested arbiter of the ideological claims of others because it is always already serving certain ideological claims. (477)

Week #8

Notes Used for 13 Oct. 1998 Seminar Meeting. –vjv

Historiography II, |||| With a Continued, Special Consideration of Dialectic/s

I do not portray being; I portray passing.
　　　　　　　　　　　　　　—An early Sophist

The world as we see it is passing.
　　　　　　　　　　　　　　—Paul of Tarsus

> Berlin, James A. "Revisionary Histories of Rhetoric: Politics, Power, and Plurality." *Writing Histories of Rhetoric* Carbondale: SIUP, 1994. 112–127

Let's return to Historiography, though I have terrible, mixed feelings about returning once ever again!, which will perhaps become clear as we proceed.

First, as someone requested last time, I need to answer the **question**, Why did I place the *CE* Ideology article between the articles in Historiography I and II? The **answer**, simply put, is that I wanted c/rudely to break up the discussion on historiography with an emphasis on Ideology and writing. Historiography is about writing history. For the most part several of us in R/C believed that our historians were practicing a "current-traditional rhetoric" in their writing history. We believed that they were not taking ideology into consideration at ALL, though ideology was taking them for all they were worth. We believed that this state of affairs needed to change. I have terrible, ambivalent feelings because I do not believe the state of affairs has changed! But I am joyfully pessimistic that they event-ually will!

In addition, I further 'plotted' the sequence of the three weeks from JB's very specific articles to his general article on historiography. I also tried to move from many people to fewer people discussing historiography. Also, note that I tried both weeks on Historiography to give you discussions (Octalog) and articles (S. Crowley and H. Kellner) that established contexts (essentialism vs. constructionism Or the parable of the death of a mother and how the three children want to remember her!) for thinking 'Historiography.' I want/ed you to see a social-epistemic exchange (large group/one person) at work on the issue of Historiography and Ideology. (Yes, I just loveeeeee long parenthetical interruptions in the middle of a sentence.) There's more, always some more, but I hope that my explanation will begin to answer the question.

Let us begin under the sign of the red ball:

I want to stop, as JB stops in his article under re/consideration, and think about summaries of what 'we' have done in historiography, and I want to stop giving for the most part mere expositions (what a joke . . . have I been doing just mere [is a French word!] expositions?)

JB begins (again) with his summary of the

> 'official' histories of rhetoric by such notables as GKennedy, EdCorbett, BVickers, WSHowell. They "depict rhetoric's historical trajectory as a march of ideas . . . characterized as unified, coherent, and rational. Rhetoric has a life of its own in the aerie realm of the intellectual firmament, transcending the play of economics and politics and power. From this lofty perch it serves as a mighty helpmate to those who would serve truth and virtue and a demystifying foe against illusion and self-interest. (112)

I wonder(ed) how the official writers of history might respond in the privacy or public/ity of their own mind to this characterization (or perhaps "redescription" [Rorty]). This summary, I can only guess, must sound really strange to them. None of the (at-the-time) living historians, as far as I know, responded to JB's characterization. The book that JB's article appeared in was dedicated, in part, to GeoKennedy. I sent him a copy. He wrote back but said nothing about any of the articles, but went on at length about some of the earlier, earlier historians, some of whom were his teachers. (How the generations pass judgment on their precursors!)

A few paragraphs later, JB reflects:

> When I encounter these reverential readings of the history of rhetoric, my first impulse, I must confess, is to resist, to portray the heroes as villains and the villains as heroes. For example, some Sophists were. . . . (114)

> But I realize my response is unjust, serving as a simple reversal of the binary oppositions on which the histories I have mentioned are formulated, oppositions repeated in more extreme forms today in our general discussions of rhetoric. Thus, the enemies of rhetoric argue that it is inherently corrupt (usually because they want to conceal or naturalize their own rhetoric) while we defenders of rhetoric too often take the opposite tack, insisting that it is inherently good. The problem with this dichotomy is that it is ahistorical. It argues that rhetoric is a practice that can somehow transcend the historical conditions of its own time, speaking in its essential purity (or, alternately, corruption) to all ages. It forgets that the formulation of a rhetoric is a product of the economic, social, and political conditions of a specific historical moment. The mission of the revisionary historian of rhetoric, I have in mind is to resist the notion of rhetoric as a unified, coherent, and univocal collection of texts stretching over time, texts that support either truth and virtue on the one hand, or error and vice on the other. The revisionary historian must instead locate the variety of rhetorics that exist at any particular moment and examine their interaction with each other and with the conditions of their production. This will require seeking out the suppressed rhetorics of women, workers, and other marginalized and silenced groups. In this study, some rhetorics will prove noble and good, but some will inevitably prove quite the contrary. (115–16)

This is still a remarkable statement, I think. When I first read it in manuscript form, I thought that Jim was setting up the opposites here as a dialectic, but he was not. He wants to back off from the . . . melodramatic (?) contraries or 'negative' deconstructions (i.e., simple reversals) and think in terms of many competing dialectical (polylectical?) exchanges.

"The mission" (image) that JB has in mind is to locate variety, if variety existed, and for sure it must have at some level—at the surface or the depths—and then to bear witness to this variety. Which would be finally interpreted to be noble or ignoble (?).

JB continues: "This synchronic investigation [however] will often lead to a diachronic one" (a "historicized one") (116). He has an excellent example of Cicero appropriating Aristotle, taking the latter as we take the latter and work him through our terministic screens, which "most reinforce our desires for our own society" (116). (Will we appropriate—have we not been appro-

> JB writes: ". . .there are always at a given moment a plurality of rhetorics, even during the most repressive times. This is hard for us to see because our traditional histories have insisted upon creating a monolithic tradition" (117). And again: "The revisionary historian of rhetoric must realize that there are also numerous rhetorics of the past that never attained enough currency in their own day to offer a serious challenge to the powerful" (117).

priating in our asides and parenthetical interruptions?—JB and play him through our own screens and screams? Was this not happening prior to his passing? Is it not found in text after text of his and of ours? But the play is different—is it not—after his passing? And what will eventually have been our passing? Dialectically?) JB gives additional examples of this synchrony to diachrony movement.

[Yes, I am being merely an expositor now, right? but will even more forthleftly break from it eventually when we get to my interests that are under attack. I generally agree with all that thoroughly-modernist JB is saying about what I called in 1987 "revisionary self-conscious historiography." It's, as I made clear then, un/just not enough to handle the problems we are confronted with. Self-consciousness requires a deep, deep, while superficial suspicion of what one says s/he needs and wants. And this suspicion needs to be worked out, while being played out, performatively, when writing histories. If only JB had been more suspicious, hermeneutically and socially suspicious! If only JB had taken the perverse insight that postmodernism is modernism. Lyotard writes: Postmodernism "is a part of the modern. All that has been received, if only yesterday (*modo, modo*, Petronius used to say), must be suspected" ("What is. . . ? in *The Postmodern Condition*, 79.)]

Continuing, JB writes: "There is a final reason for writing histories (the plural intended) along the lines drawn here—lines that are crooked and subversive [sub/versive?] of narrative peace, order, and harmony. Our search for alterity, for rhetorics other than the familiar, can reveal to us alternative possibilities in conceiving discursive practices and their power formations. . . . We must look for the dangerous other [?], the subversive silences of earlier ages and our own" (118). But un/just how dangerous? how threatening? to even the revisionary historian's agenda? We will have to wait for an answer. But it will **never include in it**, say, a reaffirmation of Showalter's hysterical fe/males in *The Female Malady* or Clement's look at Lacan's ladies in *The Lives and Legends of Jacques Lacan*. These hysterics would be too much, though terribly political subjects-cum-objects they are! They are far too hysterical, far too far Left of what is humanistically possible, given JB's acceptance of Therborn's limited notion of What is possible? limited by the negative itself. The "dangerous other" desires to express desire without any form of Negation. That's Why the other is dangerous to revisionary historians' projects. If the goal of a revisionary historian is to reinclude who was written out of history, they will have to reinclude all. Synecdochically ALL. Hysterics will break up, disrupt, the narrative, however, and will never allow for a provisional, contingent grand narrative, which JB calls for. Some more later, if I can control myselphs-as-expositor.

AND THEN JB TURNS TO HIS CRITICS:

Banish the old historians? || "But does my proposal involve a categorical refusal of other kinds of history, as some have suggested? Could I ever in my wildest flights of Leftist frenzy wish the histories of Kennedy and Corbett and Vickers and Howell be banished from consideration? I would have to answer an emphatic no to both questions" (118–19).

> "The final impression one is left with in examining Kennedy and Vickers is that their method is *unproblematically exemplary:* all that is genuinely important in pursuing the history of rhetoric has been here presented, and the reader need look no further. . . . I wish that each had been more *self-conscious* about his methods, explaining them and acknowledging their limitations" (119; emphasis added)

Did I say something earlier here that parallels this reading of K and V, but in dis/respect to JB?

Prohibit other methods? || JB: "I would also like to comment on another criticism of the position I am forwarding. As I have already indicated, my proposed historiographic method does not prohibit other methods: all it asks is that these others foreground their intentions with all their implications. If, for example, a historian decides that politics is not a part of rhetoric despite all the evidence to the contrary, then she ought to say so, explaining her reasons for taking her position. In other words, my comments are especially intended to discourage unreflective accounts—not simply accounts that disagree with my own. I am also offering, of course, what I take to be a more productive approach. . . . But of course I reserve the right to continue to criticize what I take to be their errors and inadequacies" (120).

Preclusion of normal appropriations? || JB: "I also feel constrained to make one other peace offering. I have been told at conferences (but never, to my knowledge, in print) that my recommendations would preclude the normal appropriations of historical rhetorics that are a continuing part of theory building, as Kenneth Burke has done with Aristotle. My objection is not to such uses—a necessary strategy of writing rhetorics—but to its unreflective operation" (120).

BACK TO HIS PROPOSED METHOD, with a focus on his critics:

> I would like to say a last word about the complex relation between the past and present in writing the contextualized history I am recommending. As I have suggested repeatedly, objectivity is out of the question. All historians are interested, writing their narratives from a particular ideological position. . . . My position here [once ever again!] is that the historian must acknowledge the principles—primarily ideological in nature—that are to govern this interpretation. . . . [S]he must strive to understand as much as is possible her own situatedness, primarily by realizing her decisions in writing history will be based on her own loyalties in economic, social, political, and cultural considerations. (121)

More specifically, "I would also argue that this historiographic method encourages a dialectical reading of past and present that will encourage a variety of conflicting readings, even among those who share ideological loyalties. . . . The historiographic method I am suggesting foregrounds *difference over identity*. This difference . . . is useful not simply because it offers new conceptions of the past not yet entertained. I am also convinced it offers new interpretations of the present" (122; emphasis added).

JB'S RESPONSE TO POSTMODERNism (or what I would and have called Sub/Versions and Sub/Versive Hysteriographies), an attending to the "dangerous other"?!:

JB writes: "In the closing section of this essay I want to offer a more detailed description of the historiographic method I am proposing. I want especially to address the challenge to history writing posed by the postmodern disruption in our confidence in grand historical narrative [J-F.Lyotard, *The Postmodern Condition*], a challenge that has been constantly kept in mind in what has already been said" (123). Some of what is said here, as JB reminds us, we have already read when doing "Historiography I," two weeks ago. But there are significant additions, Ones that are highly problematic. He writes:

> Against this plea for the complete and entire rejection of comprehensive historical accounts, however, I would argue for the necessity of *provisional, contingent narratives* in explaining the past and present. While history may be without an inherent plan or progression, it is the product of the complex interactions of people, social institutions, ideologies, technological conditions, and modes of production. To relinquish the comprehensive attempt to make sense of history is to risk being victimized by it. Meanwhile, those who have the most to gain from totalistic historical explanations that validate present economic and political arrangements, the most recent victors of historical battles, will continue to sponsor histories from their point of view, framing master narratives that authorize their continual power and privilege. (124; emphasis added)

This is awfully melodramatic. So the issue here is Totalization. It is true that some people have attacked Marxists such as F Jameson as espousing Totalization. How unfortunate a word.

There is Totalization and then there is Totalization. (Totalization does not necessarily = Totalitarianism.) Lyotard's project is not to attack Jameson, nor Jameson (who wrote the forward to *The Postmodern Condition*) to attack Lyotard's project. However, Jameson does find Lyotard's vision of rethinking the legitimation crisis (as a response to Habermas and the German tradition of totality) as only "protopolitical" (foreword xx). Jameson's understanding of Lyotard's heuristic of a postmodernism preceding modernism, making for ever new experimental forms of modernism is accurate.

Jameson's pointing to the Lyotard-Deleuze/Guattari is accurate. It is the case, that Lyotard, like others, do not believe in political revolution (or as Lyotard writes, in "the mutterings of the desire for a return of terror for the realization of the fantasy to seize reality [das Ding]" ("What is. . .?" in *Postmodern Condition*, 82). Lyotard does believe in the revolutionary poet's 'great, good place,' but only as a dangerous, nostalgic pull toward death itself. Instead, as Jameson characterizes, the future (post) anterior (modo) heuristic (i.e., the What will have been) is a means of holding off perpetually the nostalgic pull for a resolution into total revolution's desire for what is Not. WHAT IS NOT POSSIBLE, because predicated on THE NEGATIVE. (I would like to say something about Lyotard and the [subjectively invested] desire named Marx as expressed by Lyotard in his book *Libidinal Economy* and how it fits in, but we must move on. I have written elsewhere on this issue: see *Negation, Subjectivity, and The History of Rhetoric*, 112–21.)

> Totality can be, of course, a very problematic word. What is a totality but a set that is the achievement of Oneness as multiplicity by way of exclusion. Or What is a totality but a set that recognizes that it cannot include all things in one grand, even provisional, contingent set, but can include all things in one set among other sets, or little narratives that are in some way combined in their (political) efforts. Or a totality that is decomposed of incommensurable sets, or little narratives. There is no doubt, however, that Jameson thinks of totality as "global" or "multinational" ("Cognitive Mapping" in *Marxism and the Interpretation of Culture*. Ed. Nelson and Grossberg. Urbana: U of Illinois P, 1988. 353). And that JB would as well.

It is wonderful to see the brilliance of Jameson's understanding, while it is equally wonderful to see the brilliance of his being less than happy with Lyotard's stance toward the political as he himself (Jameson) would desire the political life. Jameson is a careful thinker. Lyotard and Jameson are of two different desires!

A TURN FOR THE WORSE, with a focus on 'provisionality':

Let us work . . . play our way back to . . . where we were before this brief excursus and bring JB into where we perhaps will have been, for JB supports his position

> *Lyotard is very Coleridgean, as Jameson suggests (foreword xviii), in relation to the problem of revolution and modernism. Lyotard is Coleridgean and a post-Marxean.* (Does this suggestion of Jameson and this statement of mine not echo back to several weeks ago, when we were interested in the question: What happens to Coleridge in JB's thinking? And What is the connection between Coleridge and Marx, dialectically?)

Spivak's readings of differences. Spivak is a far better reader and interrogator than Ebert can ever hope to be. I differ with Ebert's facile dividing practice and her lack of care.) Why then must Ebert and JB use a scapegoat to make their provisional, yet ever grand point? (I do differ with Jim's notion of a provisional grand narrative and his reading of Lyotard.)

I do know that JB had read Zavarzadeh and Co.'s work (we talked about it on several occasions) and that he was aware of what happened at Syracuse U. Perhaps, JB thinks he is being a bricoleur here, borrowing a bit of Zavarzadeh, using what is ready-at-hand for provisional ends. If so, I am still deeply troubled by his not giving us an explanation for Why he would trek with them. This is a great matter of ethos, which JB loses by associating himself with them.

But what gets me is that in closing JB writes, "The historiographic method recommended here, then, demands *honesty of the historian*, a *candid acknowledgement* of her ideological stance. . . (127)." The concepts **honesty, candid acknowledgement**, etc., are highly problematic in themselves, but when JB closes with these statements, I can only think that they do not fit at all the very person (the ethos is the style of the argument) whom he chose (chooses!) and invites us to follow.

On JB and Lyotard:

(1) JB spends no time, once again, wrestling with Lyotard and his text(s), but appeals to others thoughts.

(2) JB's borrowed notion of **provisional grand narrative(s)** is as hollow and as unproductive, perhaps counterproductive, than, the notion of **strategic essentialism**, when it was offered by Heath and Spivak and others. (Yes, I reserve the right to speak against Spivak on particular details. To speak against, as I have said repeatedly in print, is to speak not only 'contra to' but also 'alongside.'

I am a sophistic rhetorician: Everything and every thought is provisional and strategic (or tactical). What are these people . . . JB telling me? That he now wants to be rhetorical? Does he really think that he and the rest of us will be vigilant enough to make sure that 'our' now-provisional-grand narrative does not slip back into being the old Enlightenment Grand Narrative that JB and the rest of us rail against? Does he really think that he and others have that much control over language and its narrative making possibilities? Have control over "the fantasy," in the form of a provisional grand narrative, "to seize reality." Evidently, he does. I should not. What remains (thanks to the pagan gods, there are always already 'remainders" to work and play with heuristically and aleatory) . . . What remains is but to take ourselves 'through the fantasy' so as to discover repeatedly that there is Nothing, as Lacan suggests, IF we cannot totally negate the Negative, as Deleuze/Guattari suggest.

Week #9

Notes Used for 20 Oct. 1998 Seminar Meeting. –vjv

Cultural Studies I, ‖‖ With a Continued, Special Consideration of Dialectic/s

We are obviously not taking the readings for cultural studies in chronological order.

> Berlin, James A. "Cultural Studies." *Encyclopedia of Rhetoric and Composition.* Ed. Theresa Enos. NY: Garland, 1996. 154–56.

Syntax and plotting can and should be applied to someone's work, in this case, JB's. I am less interested now, this week, in the evolution of JB's motion toward and development of cultural studies; I am more interested tonight in approaching this motion and development from as many different angles and angels(-devils) as possible. These articles flow from one to the next in particular ways that are telling. Juxtaposition is everything, minus a few things that have to be got at using other techne!

Jim wanted to focus, almost exclusively but could not, on interested practitioners, that is, teachers of writing. This, I think, is admirable, though not without problems, which JB was well aware of and addressed in the third article that we will discuss this evening. (Of course, we have been discussing this problem of audience from the beginning and the problems that it poses specifically for Jim and for what he has to say to us and the profession.)

JB's entry on "cultural studies" in *The Encyclopedia of Rhetoric and Composition*, is in two parts: the general field of cultural studies and the more specific field within English departments, the teaching of rhetoric and composition. JB defines **cs** as "[t]he interdisciplinary examination of cultural texts and their effects in forming consciousness within economic and political contexts." The genus of "interdisciplinary examination" maintains **cs** as a general field and not belonging to any one department such as English.

JB, however, points to T Eagleton (more so) and J Culler (slightly less so) as noting that rhetoric can serve as "the model" for **cs** (JB 154). Then, JB sites J Trimbur and P Bizzell's work in rhetoric and composition. He mentions these four people so as to immediately make the connection between **cs** and rhetoric and composition.

Then, JB focuses on North America, saying that English departments with an interest in **cs** have worked to expand "the range of texts" and "the methods for reading and writing them" (154). The particular methods or "strategies" are from both structuralism and poststructuralism. But, JB, writes: "Most important, the construction and reception of these varied discourses are examined within the concrete economic and political contexts of their historical moment" (154).

If **cs** had a "beginning" (at least, in JB's essay) it is "by contesting the Enlightenment notion of *culture* that has historically been central to English departments." He continues:

> Culture was here regarded as an autonomous category of experience manifested in an exclusive set of canonical texts and in particular ways of reading them. These texts and interpretations were said to be universal in character and thus completely free of temporal economic and political conditions. Against this conception, cultural studies argued for an expansion of the definition of culture. Growing out of Marxist traditions as well as sociological and anthropological formulations, culture came to stand for a complex way of life, that is, the extensive patterns of behavior found in daily activities. Culture is then the entire lived experience of human agents in response to their concrete historical conditions. This definition broke down the distinction between canonical and other cultural texts, arguing that cultural workers, such as English teachers, should consider noncanonical texts and forms of representation typically excluded from concern, such as film, television, popular music, and the like. Furthermore, in a departure from orthodox Marxism, culture was to be treated as a distinct historical force that could never be reduced to a simple reflex of economic and political conditions. As the same time, it could not be altogether separated from these categories. (154–55)

Important here, I think, are the following distinctions that are not negatively, but affirmatively deconstructed (i.e., not simply reversed, but placed at a third locus or **a**locus, given whatever your ideological preference might be). For example:

Part ('High') Culture / Part ('Low') Culture Moves to Complex-Whole (All of Culture) Way of Life

The movement is
- from part/part (metonymic)

- to parts/whole (synecdochic)
- to [whole/whole] (ironic).

This my explanation (appropriation and intervention), however, would be problematic for Jim. The [whole/whole] (ironic) would be fine for him IF interpreted as K Burke does in his *Grammar of Motives*, specifically in the appendix, "The Four Master Tropes." The [whole/whole] (ironic) would not be fine for him IF interpreted as a radical poststructuralist, perhaps Lyotardian Postmodern, reading. I think—and of course this is my guess—Jim would have found much in Lyotard's book *Discourses, figure* that he could use productively and sympathetically, while finding much that would horrify him. (Jim borrowed **parts**, as we all do, but borrowed *as if* not taking also what he thought he left behind in the very **part** he took with him into writing his articles and into teaching his classes. I will return to this issue later—perhaps during the Retrospective—and specifically what I mean by it and its importance.)

In the paragraph—following that quoted above—JB writes:

> Cultural studies has also been strongly shaped by feminist theory, by African-American studies and by gay and lesbian studies. As a result of these multiple and complex influences, cultural studies has commonly come to be seen as the study of signifying practices in the formation of subjectivities within concrete economic, social, and political conditions. These practices range from the activities of the family, the school, the workplace, and the peer group to the more familiar behavior associated with the cultural sphere, such as the arts and the media and their modes of production and consumption. . . . In short, wherever signifying practices are shaping consciousness in daily life, cultural studies has work to do. (155)

Which is everywhere.

JB ends with a brief paragraph specifically directed to what is to happen in terms of **cs** in English departments. I will take but a couple of startling, but appropriate sentences: "Significantly, the classroom will replace research publications as the center of the discipline. Here teachers and students will develop methods for reading and writing cultural codes, and these codes will cut across the aesthetic, the economic, the political, the philosophical, and the scientific" (155–56). Hence: previously the relationship was, and still is in most cases, *publication/teaching*, with the first privileged; he predicts a reversal, *research in the classroom/research in the library*. What is being said here, among other things, is that both teachers and students will enact their *praxes* (critical thought and critical action) together in the 'class' room as a form of research and publication. These sentences are perfect for a transition into a discussion of (JB's defense) of Paulo Freire.

I say JB's "defense," for his is a response to the interviewers of PF, who find fault with Freire's pedagogy not being use-(value)-able in the U.S., and thereby become themselves and only encourage others to be sectarians. (The interview was published in *JAC*.) JB sees, as others elsewhere see, PF as "reading and writing the world." What does this mean?

> Berlin, James A. "Freirean Pedagogy in the U.S.: A Response." *Journal of Advanced Composition* 12 (Fall 1992): 414–21.

Many things. JB writes: "Freire provides a rich rationale to support those who argue that literacy ought not be treated as a merely instrumental 'skill,' a useful tool in the mastery of more significant and substantive academic subjects. For Freire, to learn to read and write is to learn to name the world, and in this naming is found a program for understanding the conditions of our experience and, most important, for acting in and on them" (414).

This is a very aesthetically and politically pleasing statement: "in this naming is found a program for understanding the conditions of our experience [the conditions for the possibilities] and, most important, for acting in and on them." Yes, I repeat it, for it bears ever being repeated.

(I don't want to freak you out, my fellow students, into thinking that I am crossing over now to side with JB completely, leaving behind all that JB leaves behind in relation to poststructuralism and postmodernism. I am leaving *nothing* behind. I say, "Yes, I repeat it," for it states where I, too, begin but then cannot not add what JB and PF would leave behind in the name of 'we want no sectarian determinism in our thinking.' The word is not my word, 'sectarian'; there is *nothing* privileged in this word to describe the world I live in and the world in which I **think** change and action (praxis). I guess that every -ism has to have a devil's term that will segregate the unclean, those who would disrupt the task at hand. That would give up 'hope' as the particular group would have hope. As I say: "I am leaving *nothing* behind." My creative-political act is to say No to Nothing, while affirming, but an affirming by(e) way a non-positive affirmation (Foucault). I may be 'contra to' (against) stopping where JB must stop; I may be 'along side' (against) and then may be a moving on from where JB stopped. Yes, I am 'against' JB. I find more de-naming/d-territorializing to do. [Some more later.])

JB summarizes the same notions that he has previously summarized repeatedly about language. This, too, are PF's notions of language, which is that it constitutes the world, but does not fatally, unhopefully determine our places in it.

JB writes about PF's vision of education:

> For democracy to function . . . citizens must actively engage in public debate, applying reading and writing practices in the service of articulating their positions and their critiques

of the positions of others. The inability of citizens to write and read for the public forum thus defeats the central purpose of democracy: to ensure that all interests are heard before a communal decision is made.

Freire relates this silencing of citizens through literacy education to the formation of subjects as agents. Without the language to name our experience, we are the instruments of the language of others. As I am authorized through active literacy to name the world as I experience it (not as others tell me I should experience it), I become capable of taking action, of assuming control of my environment. In more direct terms, literacy enables the individual to understand that the conditions of experience are made by human agents and thus can be remade by human agents. This process of making and remaking, furthermore, is conducted in communities, in social collections. For Freire, however, the individual must never be sacrificed to any group-enforced norm (as he underscores in this interview). All voices must be heard and considered in taking action, and the integrity of the individual must never be compromised" (417)

JB continues by focusing ever more on the classroom:

> Years of enduring the banking model of education have taken their toll so that, like the unschooled peasants that Freire tells us about, our students often refuse to speak. They would rather sit quietly and take notes that they later will reproduce exactly for the exam. When pressed to active dialogue, they frequently deny the obvious social and political conflicts they enact and witness daily. For example, the majority of male students I have encountered at Purdue have in our first discussions assured me that race and gender inequalities no longer exist in the U.S. and simply do not merit further discussion. And inequalities that do remain, they insist, are only apparent injustices since they are the result of inherent and thus unavoidable features of human nature (women are weaker and more emotional than men, for example), or are the product of individual failure (most homeless people refuse to work hard and so choose to live in the street.)

> It is at the moment of denial that the role of the teacher as problem poser is crucial, providing methods for the questioning that locates the points of conflict and contradiction. These methods most often require a focus on the language students invoke in responding to their experience. The teacher attempts to supply students with heuristic strategies for decoding their characteristic ways of representing the world. . . . The methods of questioning that the teacher poses are designed to reveal the contradictions and conflicts inscribed in the very language of students' thoughts and utterance. (417–18)

JB closes his 'response' with a brief discussion of "Freirean Pedagogy in the U.S." His prime example (of our failure in the U.S.) is what happened [at the Battle] at UT-Austin, where a majority of faculty voted in favor of "restructur[ing] the required freshman composition course as a class in writing about cultural differences, including race, gender, class, and ethnic designation. Despite the strong support of the English department for this offering, a vocal minority of faculty members within as well as outside the department protested, enlisting the support of former Texas [in Austin] students in pressuring the university president and college dean to ban the course." (420). As we well know now, the vote was overturned by the administration. He writes: "The nation that prides itself on being the most free and democratic country in the world (as Reagan repeatedly reminded us) has somehow spawned a group of intellectuals who balk at the idea that a course in rhetoric might encourage students to exercise actively their rights and responsibilities as citizens in a democracy" (420).

JB's strategy becomes clearer when he writes these final sentences: "And so Freire is installed as Secretary of Education in Sao Paulo, democracy is established in much of Eastern Europe, and a course in cultural differences at the University of Texas is postponed—indefinitely. The more things change abroad, the more they remain repressively the same at home."

Though JB only makes passing reference to the TX course as one in the U.S., he does focus on the required writing course at Purdue, in his article that we will consider now, which is a course that he considers to be an incipient success. (I am inferring he sees it as a success, for he does not talk about its failures, if any; I am inferring success also because he offers it as an example.)

> Berlin, James A. "Poststructuralism, Cultural Studies, and the Composition Classroom." *Rhetoric Review* 11 (Fall 1992): 16–33. Rpt. Professing the New Rhetoric. Ed. Theresa Enos and Stuart C. Brown. Englewood Cliffs, New Jersey: Prentice Hall, 1994. 461–480.

JB enters the article by making it clear that the exigency for his writing this article has been brought about by a number of specific articles and conversations (Burkean Parlor) published in *RR* as well as other journals. His discussion, he tells us, will deal with how the audience (readers) have responded to postmodern prose and specifically to postmodern prose that is to explain this prose; will deal with how "postmodern conceptions are counterparts to discussions in social-epistemic rhetoric" (17). He continues: "My intent is to demonstrate that the complexities of theory have immediate pedagogical applications, and that one of the efforts of composition teachers must be to discover these. Indeed, I will argue that the merger of theory and classroom practice in a uniquely new relation is one of the results of (what I should perhaps now call) postmodern rhetorical theory" (17).

What JB does is to give a lengthy summary of some of the basic features of the postmodern in relation to "the status of the subject; the characteristics of signifying practices; the role of master theories in explaining human affairs" (18). I don't want to rehearse any of this, for all of you have taken more than your fair share of courses in which these features are discussed. And again, I don't want to summarize what JB has to say about 'social-epistemic rhetoric,' which by now, surely you understand. Remember that this article of Jim's is aimed precisely at an audience of teachers of writing and of graduate students who are not familiar with the features of either -ism. I want instead to focus on JB's and his students' course(s) at Purdue:

He writes:

> Our main concern is the relation of current signifying practices to the structuring of subjectivities—of race, class, and gender formation, for example—in our students and ourselves. The effort is to make students aware of cultural codes, the competing discourses that are influencing their formations as the subjects of experience. Our larger purpose is to encourage students to resist and to negotiate these codes—these hegemonic discourses—in order to bring about more democratic and personally humane economic, social, and political arrangements. From our perspective, only in this way can they become genuinely competent writers and readers. (27)

He continues:

> It is our hope that students who can demystify the subtle devices of persuasion in these cultual codes will be motivated to begin the re-forming of subjectivities and social arrangements, a re-forming which is a normal part of democratic political arrangements. We also want to explore the wide range of codes that students confront daily—print, film, television—in order to prepare them to critique their experiences with these codes. (27)

The course has six units:

> **advertising**
> **work**
> **play**
> **education**
> **gender**
> **Individuality**.

Each of these units, ... **oops, a break . . .**

> **Note:** The methodology being used is close to but not identical with the methodology outlined by Freire in his *Pedagogy of the Oppressed* (85–105), in which those in the 'culture circles' are to begin with a 'thematic universe' and then look for and eventually with 'generative themes.' Which would be a primary theme such as 'Domination.' Which, in turn, has as its opposite the term 'Liberation.' Hence the binary, Domination/Liberation. Moving from these large abstractions, the peasants in the culture circles are to begin coding and then decoding to see what has been, heretofore, lost to their eyes, their minds, their thinking and, most important, their speaking with others. It is in the 'speaking' that Freire sees the realization of Liberation, what he calls "ontological vocation" (Being calling us) to become Free.
>
> As the circle continues, methods of ethnography are employed with ethnographers practicing ethnography on ethnographers.
>
> There is a step that JB does not mention in his course and that is a second stage that requires the "investigators" to go into the village (West Lafayette?) to construct sympathetic descriptions "towards what they see." These are recorded in their notebooks. The group develops a report. There is an evaluation meeting, with an exchange of various reports and then counter-reports proposed. There is a chance, after discussions, to revise the original reports. All of this is done so as to locate contradictions, which are "limit situations," which are to be overcome.

A Limit Situation: PF writes: "In one of the thematic investigations carried out in Santiago, a group of tenement residents discussed a scene showing a drunken man walking on the street and three young men conversing on the corner. The group participants commented that "the only one there who is productive and useful to his country is the souse who is returning home after working all day for low wages and who is worried about his family because he can't take care of their needs. He is the only worker. He is a decent worker and a souse like us" (111). PF continues: "There are two important aspects to these declarations. On the one hand, they verbalize the connection between earning low wages, feeling exploited, and getting drunk—getting drunk as a flight from reality, as an attempt to overcome the frustration of inaction, as an ultimately self-destructive solution. On the other hand, they manifest the need to rate the drunkard highly. He is the 'only one useful to his country, because he works, while the others only gab.' After praising the drunkard, the participants then identify themselves with him, as workers who also drink—'decent workers'" (111–12).

As if a heading in a critical studies anthology, has a group of readings. JB tells us, "The unit on education includes an analysis of US schools by a diverse range of observers: William Bennett, Jonathon Kozol, John Dewey, and James Thurber" (27).

Following the readings is a film or video that parallel the readings.

JB, tells us, however, "The important consideration is not the texts in themselves but the texts in relation to certain methods of interpreting them" (27). In other words, the use of coding and then decoding similar to that used by the early R Barthes. But more importantly as that reported by PF in his *Pedagogy of the Oppressed*. (See right yellow box.) Students are asked, specifically, to look for key terms and then to place them in their binary (full) terms. For example, in the essay "The Days of a Cowboy are Marked by Danger, Drudgery, and Low Pay" from *The Wall Street Journal*. In searching for key terms, students note(d) the use of such terms as

> [owners]
> Cowboss
> cowboss's wife
> cowboys

Upon close inspection, when doing coding and decoding, the students come to see that in the article the "meaning of 'cowboss' is established by seeing it in binary opposition to the cowboys who work for him as well as the owners who work away from the ranch in cities. At other times in the essay the cowboss is grouped together with the cowboys in opposition to office workers. Through the description of labor relations on the ranch, the cowboys are also situated in contrast to urban union workers, but the latter are never explicitly mentioned. Finally, the exclusively masculine nature of ranching is suggested only at the end of the essay when the cowboss's wife is described in passing as living apart from the ranch on the cowboss's own small spread, creating male/female domain binary. All of these binaries suggest others, such as the opposition of nature/civilization, country/city, cowboy/urban cowboy, and the like. Students begin to see that these binaries are arranged hierarchically, with one term privileged over the other. They also see how unstable these hierarchies can be, however, with a term frequently shifting valences as it moves from one binary to another—for example, cowboy/union worker but cowboss/cowboy." (28)

Once the analysis (key terms, coding binaries and hierarchies, and decoding them) has been accomplished, the students then further analyze, discuss and write about them. When students write they are renaming, rewriting the world, as JB speaks of what Freire calls for. It is the production of these new texts and sets of more democratic relationships (no one privileged in a static formation, no hierarchy fixed) that students learn that situations that dehumanize can be renamed and rewritten so that they will rehumanize.

The word is "hope." The question is IF students learn how to perform the kind of *praxis* that JB and his fellow (grad) students are asking students to perform, then there will be social change.

JB straightforwardly writes: "It is our hope that students who can demystify the subtle devices of persuasion in these cultural codes will be motivated to begin the re-forming of subjectivities and social arrangements, a re-forming which is a normal part of democratic political arrangements" (27). Another question forever remains that JB had articulated but not in print as far as I know. (He read a paper at the *Marxist Literary Group* in Pittsburgh—we were on the panel together—in which he raised this question and illustrated it with a particular student in mind.) Why is it that some students learn to code and decode so as to understand how they are being manipulated by advertisements into becoming consumers of what they do not need at all and then write papers of renaming the world, making it a better place, and do an excellent job of it, BUT then go out and let themselves be manipulated all over again by buying the very object that they had supposedly renamed in their class *praxis*?

Such activity expressed in this at last haunting question leads but to cynicism. (I will discuss this as fully as I can during the Retrospective. I have discussed it in a paper delivered, as a plenary speaker, to the Research Network Forum, CCCC, 1998.)

Week #10

Notes Used for 27 Oct. 1998 Seminar Meeting. –vjv

Cultural Studies II, |||| With an Ever-Growing Concern for Cynicism, or What I Would Call Now the Dialectic/s of Cynicism:

> *. . . we must make no mistake about ourselves: we are as much automaton as mind. . . . Proofs only convince the mind; habit provides the strongest proofs and those that are most believed. It inclines the automaton, which leads the mind unconsciously along with it."*
>
> —Pascal, Pensee

Let's re/begin by taking a look at the language in the first paragraph of JB's and Vivion's Introduction to *Cultural Studies in the English Classroom*. The title of the section is "A Provisional Definition," which strongly suggests that this **is** to be the subject of interest.

> Berlin, James A., and Michael J. Vivion. "Introduction" to *Cultural Studies in the English Classroom.* Ed. *James A. Berlin and Michael J. Vivion. Portsmouth, NH: Boynton/Cook Heinemann, 1992. vii-xvi.*

And it is. However, I would ask you to look at the ending of the first paragraph: "That this 'best' is nothing other than an ideological designation—as its vociferous support by the likes of William Bennett and Gary Wills makes clear—[that] remains unacknowledged" (vii). While the keyword may be "provisional," the other keyword for me is "unacknowledged." For JB, these are both very important words. Let's just recall without going into any details JB's compromise of going with "provisional grand narratives." And let's just recall that the primary difference between traditional historians and revisionary (social-epistemic) historians is that while traditional historians un/just gather the facts and spin a tale, the revisionary historians 'acknowledge' their ideological slants in rendering history. The latter, of course, is preferred ideologically over the former. I can agree to this assumption and have espoused it continually, but with major reservations that 'necessitate' a sub/version of them, which is another story for another time.

But let's back up here some and systematize our thinking. And in this way:

Traditional historians or discussants about English departments and the values that should inform them (after all, this is the issue in the opening paragraph of the "Introduction" that we are examining) such as "William Bennett and Gary Wills" (vii) **say what they say without knowing what they say**. Why? Because their "ideological designation . . . remains unacknowledged" (vii). As Marx says, "They do this without being aware of it" (*Capital 1*, 166–67, trans. Ben Fowkes. Vintage).

Žižek states it so well just as Tom Rickert will in his forthcoming dissertation:

> The very concept of ideology implies a kind of basic, constitutive *naivete*: The misrecognition of its own presuppositions, of its own effective conditions, a distance, a divergence between so-called social reality and our distorted representation, our false consciousness of it. That is why such a 'naive consciousness' can be submitted to a critical-ideological procedure. The aim of this procedure is to lead the naive ideological consciousness to a point at which it can recognize its own effective conditions, the social reality that it is distorting, and through this very act dissolve itself. In the more sophisticated versions of the critics of ideology—that developed by the Frankfurt School, for example—it is not just a question of seeing things (that is, social reality) as they 'really are,' of throwing away the distorting spectacles of ideology; the main point is to see how the reality itself cannot reproduce itself without this so-called ideological mystification. The mask is not simply hiding the real state of things; the ideological distortion is written into its very essence. (*The Sublime Object of Ideology* 28).

It can be argued, therefore, that the ideological distortion functions intentionally, heuristically. What is wanted (as both Marx and Freud had paved the way in terms of what Ricoeur calls "the hermeneutics of suspicion" and as JB has said in his Freirean way), then is a counter interventional device or counter heuristic to open up the conditions for the possibility of demystification.

Revisionary (social-epistemic) historians or discussants about English departments and the values that should inform them such as JB and Michael Vivion. . . . Can I finish this sentence/claim? Should I? Ought I? What might be on the other side, IF there is another side, or mask to strip away or What might there be hiding, not simply hiding? Above: "The mask is not simply hiding the real state of things; the ideological distortion is written into its very essence." This is a troubling, deeply troubling problem/atic posed here by Žižek. If this is so problematic, should we not deal with it. If this 'beginning' reading of What is to fall is compelling, Should we venture into areas that will strip away even 'revisionary (social-epistemic) thinking'? And thereby strip away hope?

There is a certain lived, experiential truth to the power of 'critique.' Once we begin critiquing we can never stop the force of critique itself continuing on its own critiquing the conditions of critique. Yes, self reflexiveness kicks in, biting itself on the tail as well as perpetually (not provisionally) kicking itself on the tail! It is no longer a question, therefore, Should we?, Ought we?, for 'critique' itself **will do it to us while it knows it is doing it without any hope**, but taking us cynically through the fantasy of never being able to reach the sublime object (being home).

What am I pointing to so ahead of myself in this discussion, what am I seeing in the distance?

Too simply put, that while JB and MV point to "unacknowledged ideology" as the problem that must be finally acknowledged by traditional or foundationalist thinkers so as to stop advocating and practicing an epistemology that can but hurt students in our classrooms, JB as well as MV do not see, cannot bring themselves to seeing, that they themselves have an unacknowledged ideology that leads but to cynicism. This, then, would be What I am 'provisionally' pointing to. And with regrets.

First of all, it has to be understood that I am **not** saying, therefore, Let us not critique the Bill Bennetts of the world! Let us un/just stay in our mystified states and un/just enjoy our symptoms as we attempt to reach for the sublime object. This, indeed, would be but another form of a terrible cynicism that would open the doors to the worst nightmares of political fascism.

Secondly, it has to be understood Why I am questioning not only the Bill Bennetts but also the JBs. And the VVs. Let us look at Žižek's formulation of the question/problematic. (I have previously in excruciating detail taken readers through step by step analyses of What we call critical thinking and action, say, in "An After/word: Preparing to Meet the 'Faces' that We will have Met," which still has no reader[s]. I have anecdotally in the simplest of prose taken the listeners to the point of real/izing that there is reason to doubt the value of cultural studies and its ways of critique and that JB himself did publicly in front of the MLG, only to be told by my audience that I merely wanted to shock them, raise their ire. Perhaps I am no longer the person who can say these things. And therefore, I am but Left with the question: Is all that is Left—far left of what it is to be humanistically possible—**is** to be locked in our cells of silence by the authorities, authoritative audiences, and while there, practice our music? Or is there not still another option that we must but repeat and repeat and repeat as our obsessive insights un/just as the ancient mariner cannot but do. (I have not forgotten Coleridge. Have you?) But, But, But. . . . A per/verse game that can be played by all sides. And there is always the Baudriardean "fatal strategies." We have all un/kinds of antibiotics Left until finally the Sublime Object has its revenge on us.)

Let's return to Žižek, where he far Left off:

> "We find . . . the paradox of a being which can reproduce itself only in so far as it is misrecognized and overlooked: the moment we see it 'as it really is,' this being dissolves itself into nothingness or, more precisely, it changes into another kind of reality. That is why we must avoid the simple metaphors of demasking, of throwing away the veils which are supposed to hide the naked reality. . . .
>
> But all this is already well known: it is the classic concept of ideology as 'false consciousness,' misrecognition of the social reality which is part of this reality itself. Our question is: Does this concept of ideology as a naive consciousness still apply to today's world? Is it still operating today? In the *Critique of Cynical Reason,* a great bestseller in Germany . . . Peter Sloterdijk puts forward the thesis that ideology's dominant mode of functioning is cynical, which renders impossible—or, more precisely, vain—the classic critical-ideological procedure. The cynical subject is quite aware of the distance between the ideological mask and the social reality, but he none the less still insists upon the mask. The formula, as proposed by Sloterdijk, would then be: **'they know very well what they are doing, but still, they are doing it.'** Cynical reason is no longer naive, but is a paradox of an enlightened false consciousness: one knows the falsehood very well, one is well aware of a particular interest hidden behind an ideological universality [cum provisionality], but still one does not renounce it.
>
> WE must distinguish this cynical position strictly from what Sloterdijk calls *kynicism.* . . ." (28–29; emphasis added)

. . . to which we will eventually return. Some day.

Before going on I want to look again and quickly at the close of the paragraph: "That this 'best' is nothing other than an ideological designation—as its vociferous support by the likes of William Bennett and Gary Willis makes clear—remains unacknowledged. And this brings us to **the subject** of cultural studies." This is a strange almost pathological sentence. My questions: Why do JB and MV use these strawmen to pivot into their discussions? Why do they use the phrase "nothing other than an ideological designation"? What are the other options? To admit it? and then the ideological designation will be more properly *such a thing* but one that of course JB and MV would not agree with? Why the words 'vociferous' and 'by the likes of' (as if Ben/Gary were lepers!?)? Why are these subjects . . . I mean objects . . . being kicked? We who would be readers of the book would already be predisposed against them! Why do the editors then think that we would want them to kick Bennett and Willis? There's something pathological here. It makes me want to ask, Are these **the subject/s**, as suggested transitionally, of cultural studies who would kick?

Now does any of this apply to JB? I ask you.

I still think that the best article on cultural studies that Jim wrote is ". . .Collapsing Boundaries." In it, he connects

> Eagleton and Johnson's work
> with his own work in terms of 'social-epistemic' rhetoric
> and then with others' work.

He makes a good case for the movement of English departments, during the last 100 years, toward cultural studies.

> Berlin, James A."Composition Studies and Cultural Studies: Collapsing Boundaries." *Into the Field: Sites of Composition Studies.* Ed. Anne Ruggles Gere. NY: MLA, 1993. 99–116

There was in 1992–1993 a critical mass of cultural studies theorists and practitioners. Today, there're even more. As Jim Sosnoski last told me, "cultural studies is a hot topic." It is creating its own market. Notice how people are jumping on the bandwagon. Each publishing house is looking ever again for the next hot textbook or scholarly book advocating cultural studies. Many departments are looking to hire a cultural studies person.

Cultural studies is, indeed, moving into dangerous times.

Is it clear by now that I have said two things: The basic principles of **cs** are in danger of leading both its teachers and students toward cynicism; and its critical, market success is in danger of leading **cs** toward being totally appropriated by kapitalism. There is no sign of either of these possibilities being thought about, mused over, by JB and Co. in terms of Do they/Will they (i.e., the conditions for cynicism/appropriation) exist? Will they be good or bad? Are they possible? None of these suspicions at all! This is all so disconcerting.

The 'reflexivity' always talked about by JB as well as Richard Johnson is not practiced in relation to cynicism and appropriation, which are finally the same. Cultural studies is becoming a success. "Cultural studies is a hot topic." Therefore, if not practiced by those who would advocate cultural studies, then some of us will have had to continue to practice a cultural-studies that **is** reflexive. (We are told again on pp. 100–101 that 'subjects' have become 'objects' of study, with the old subject-as-foundation being gone. How far gone? Removed? Has it been merely moved from one [right] pocket to one [left] pocket?) Let us call the critical activity not 'resistance postmodernism' as **cs** (ebert, JB) but 'reflexive postmodernism' as **cs**. (Is 'reflexive' similar to the pariah called 'ludic postmodernism'? Perhaps so. It was never been demonstrated, merely announced by Zavarzadeh, Mortin, and Ebert, that such postmodernists as Derrrida and Ulmer, Spivak and Haraway—and let us not forget P. DeMan—were merely ludic. DeMan reminded us perpetually that demystification was one of the most dangerous myths of all!)

It is not necessary to invent or to recapture historically what has been deflected; it is only necessary and most desirable to accept all that JB and Co. have thrown out or deflected in the name of maintaining critical integrity for the 'subject' that would presume to critique while 'it itself' is constituted by language. Therefore, we must, we cannot but, go back and reinclude all that was, e.g., unacceptable in and about Foucault and disincorporation. It is a necessity and most desirable to live in the paradox.

I want to turn now to what I consider to be another offer to us all—and to JB—to embrace CYNICISM.

I am referring to a position taken by Pat Bizzell in her article on a return to rhetorical authority.

> Bizzell, Patricia. "Beyond Anti-Foundationalism to Rhetorical Authority: Problems Defining 'Cultural Literacy.'" *College English* 52.6 (Oct 1990): 661–75.

It is crucial to realize my point before we begin to separate each other out into camps that will not be able to hear-listen to each other. My point will be that with the end of naive Foundationalism and naive Essentialism and with the substitute stand-in of what is variously called 'strategic essentialism' and 'provisionary grand narratives' come eventually the beginning of naive and sophisticated cynicism. There comes an eternal night of black vs. white, yet at times gray, Modernism. One of the criticisms of poststructuralism and postmodernism is that each is cynical since each is not founded on any notion of reaching the truth. The idea of consensus as the new 'truth' is also, given the available arguments, cynical. Even consensus with heavy, heavy doses of radical dissensus such as that I have attempted to practice can be seen as cynical. Since God, now dead, is no longer a tenable super-Subject but only a sublime Object, HE has his revenge in telling us all (debunks) that we are but mere Cynics. If we no longer believe in God the Object, this God will believe in and for us, none the less! As Marx, who started much of this critique stuff said so eloquently when he talks about the opposition of persons (subjects) and things (objects), Human beings no longer believe, but their commodities (things, objects) believe for them. (See Žižek 34–35. See Vitanza "on Objects," *CCC* 1998.)

In the light or darkness of these arguments, We—all the God's or gods' children—are none the less cynical. Therefore, understand that I am not picking on any one person or group as being cynical; I am instead pointing to the very conditions of a variety of possible cynicisms. Also, understand that I do not capitulate to this charge and fall into total misery; after all has been said and undone, there are other options to remaining in cynicism! To which I will eventually return. For now, let's look at Bizzell.

PB globally in the article establishes her antithetical-dialectical context for the problem of reclaiming rhetorical authority by way of the differences between *foundational* and *antifoundational* presuppositions in relation to literacy. Her personages, e.g., are, on the one hand, E. D. Hirsch, and, on the other, Richard Rorty. For the first, truth is found not made; for the second, truth is made not found. (I'm sorry. Of course, we know this, but the context speaks to the audience and is well-worth reviewing again, with its purpose, I hope, becoming clear as we proceed here.) PB speaks of 'transcendental authority' and 'rhetorical authority.' While the foundationalists feel no pain when they say something is True or has ahistorical value in itself and should, ought to be studied, the anti-foundationalists feel glee when they hear such a statement because it allows them to make the critique that the judgments are historical and bound by the accidents of race, gender, class, and politics (666–67). But the anti-foundationalists also feel pain, for they can offer, Bizzell claims, no absolute except 'there are no absolutes' which itself as a claim is open to accidents.

Bizzell sees a problem, a problem that is often pointed to by both foundationalists and anti-anti-foundationalists (and there is a difference between the two): She points to the contradictory situation that anti-foundationalist find themselves in when arguing against a fixed and select canon and arguing for adding 'difference' as a criterion instead of 'the best that was thought and writ, etc.' as the criterion for selection. PB writes:

> If one does not happen to share the interests of these groups [Hirsch et al. foundationalists] why should one respond to their claims [in the first place]? Anti-foundationalist philosophers cannot answer this question because they cannot without logical inconsistency claim to possess any values to the authority of which anyone else should bow nor any knowledge anyone else should regard as true. . . . Anti-foundationalist critics sometimes try to get out of this bind by arguing that they want a pluralistic canon simply so that the nature of difference can be studied. . . . Apparently, it does not matter what we read, so long as it is unfamiliar. By this logic, while white men should be reading work by women and ethnic minorities, women and ethnics should be studying the traditional canon. . . .

I think there is a sort of pedagogical bad faith in this position. We tell the students we are only teaching them about difference. Yet in order to do that, we must deconstruct ideologies the students hold as foundational, a very painful process that students often oppose no matter how egalitarian and non-authoritarian the teacher tries to be. For example, James Berlin has designed an experimental course to replace traditional freshman composition at Purdue University. His course asks students to deconstruct dominant ideologies on relation between the sexes and between employers and workers. Berlin has found that students hold firmly to the ideologies they are supposed to question. Women and men defend prostitution as a woman's right to make money any way she sees fit; and they explain unjustified pay cuts, unsafe working conditions, and other oppressive job situations which they have experienced as 'good lessons' that toughen them and so will help them get ahead in the future.

Berlin's account makes me wonder what he can offer to students to make it worth their while to bear with the painful deconstructive process he asks of them. It seems to me that Berlin, and many of the rest of us who try to make a pluralistic study of difference into a curriculum, are calling students to the service of some higher good which we do not have the courage to name. We exercise authority over them in asking them to give up their foundational beliefs, but we give them nothing to put in the place of these foundational beliefs because we deny the validity of all authority, including, presumably, our own." (669–70; emphasis added)

It is important to see that Bizzell is relying on the principle of non-contradiction, which of course JB does as well. The argument that she brings against these so-called anti-foundationalist is a pseudo-commonplace argument that lives on in its death.

There are two basic problems with the argument being applied here: (a) It begs a question and thereby creates the conditions for establishing what Lyotard calls a *differend*. There is absolutely no justification for using this argument since the language game of formal or informal logic are held in question, suspicion, at the very beginning of the discussion. (There would have to be a third outside place to make a judgment between Found-Antifound.) Very much on the contrary, anti-foundationalists should answer the question posed by foundationalist and in doing so enter into a bearing witness to the differend that has been constructed and to attempt to discover or invent new idioms for the differend (see Lyotard, *The Differend: Phrases in Dispute*); (b) However, if the anti-foundationalists were to close their eyes to this fallacy of use and admit the pseudo-argument and all the rules of logic, then they could counterargue that the so-called contradiction in the use of a term is nothing but an equivocation and therefore there is no contradiction whatsoever. These stupid commonplace pseudo-arguments such as 'not to act is nonetheless to act' are all examples of subtle shifts in meaning (in this case, shifts in the meaning of the word 'act').

Bizzell continues into the cynical moment of a *synthesis* (inviting JB and us to follow) but attempts to ameliorate it somewhat. She writes:

> To take the next step in our rhetorical turn, we will have to be more forthright about the ideologies we support as well as those we attack, and we will have to articulate a positive program legitimated by an authority that is nevertheless non-foundational. [Notice that PB does not say 'anti-foundational.'] We must help our students, and our fellow citizens, to engage in a rhetorical process that can collectively generate trustworthy knowledge and beliefs conducive to the common good—knowledge and beliefs to displace the repressive ideologies an unjust social order would inscribe in the skeptical void.
>
> Perhaps a way to begin the rhetorical process would be to aver provocatively that we intend to make our students better people, that we believe education should develop civic virtue. . . .
>
> I am suggesting that we must be equally forthright in avowing the ideologies that motivate our teaching and research. For example, in the case of James Berlin's course at Purdue University which I described earlier, Berlin and his fellow instructors might stop trying to be value-neutral and anti-authoritarian in the classroom. Berlin tells his students that he is a Marxist but disavows any intention of persuading them to his point of view. Instead, he might openly state that this course aims to promote values of sexual equality and left-oriented labor relations and that this course will challenge students' values insofar as they conflict with these aims. Berlin and his colleagues might openly exert their authority as teachers to try to persuade students to agree with their values instead of pretending that they are merely investigating the nature of sexism and capitalism and leaving students to draw their own conclusions.
>
> But wouldn't Berlin then be a propagandist? What is the legitimate authority of teachers, or any other orators? I would argue that this authority is derived from ideologies that already have some currency in the community the orators or teachers serve. Not everyone in America is against sexism, for example, but an argument against sexism can make use of values concerning human equality and fair play that even some sexists may hold. **In other words, the orator can point out that a contradiction exists among the values that people hold and try to persuade them to rectify it in favor of the values the orator supports. The orator can urge, don't believe in both equality and sexism; give up the sexism. Thus the oratorical exercise of authority does recommend a positive position but does not impose it.** The orator tries to achieve a consensus around the change in ideologies he or she advocates, but a consensus can only be achieved through collective participation in the rhetorical process." (671–73; emphasis added)

I agree that Jim needs to step straight forward and announce what he intends to do and not worry about keeping his distance and letting students decide for themselves. What he is allegedly reporting—this article is not in print so as to verify these paraphrases—is strange yet wonderful in that he is expressing doubts, which I mentioned that he had expressed at the MLG. I wonder if these two supposed different papers are the same paper.

There's much that I find problematic with Pat's strategy in the article on rhetoric authority.

1. The selection of *Profession 88* and the MLA authors as representatives of anti-foundationalism can only be for the purposes of selecting a straw person argument. They are MLA! They are Literature people! They are a bunch of criticism people who only end up forever suppressing and politically oppressing us-teachers of writings! So goes the mind of cynicism ticking off the negative points, which don't need to be ticked off; so goes the mind of cynicism turning the prayer wheel that, as object, will pray for (prey on) us. These people are not representative of any group that we 'could' take seriously or playfully such as the group of Derrida and Spivak. The authors' understanding of anti-foundationalism in *P 88* is so sophomoric that it cannot be used as an understanding of anti-foundationalism that we could take as support that could advance Pat's claim. It only backfires on Pat, while it propels her unknowingly.

2. The continual use of the heuristic of finding contradictions is presented in the most non-problematic way, which JB himself does. What is so essential and necessary about the principle of noncontradiction? Why would a feminist use this principle without some explanation when so many feminists are fundamentally critical of its use 'against' them (see Nancy Jay, "Gender and Dichotomy." *Feminist Studies* 7.1 [1981]: 38–56; Andrea Nye, *Words of Power* NY: Routledge, 1990.) Moreover, why would Pat call these problems contradictions (a word from philosophical rhetoric) instead of paradoxes (rhetoric) or of mixed feelings (psychology)?

3. At times, so-called contradictions work for us in the best of pragmatic ways. It is important at times to situate ourselves in the promise of a paradox. Totally excluding the heuristic of accepting contradictions can rule out its beneficial side. And yet (perversely), if we insist on relying on the principle of noncontradiction as a means of exclusion, it will put us in the double pleasurable bond of not just being sadistic towards others but masochistic towards ourselves.

4. Pointing out contradictions—the only method that Pat's offers—in people's (students') thinking is not a very effective method of changing the minds of resistant-stubborn people. This method will only in many cases reinforce their bigotry, making the students un/just that more reactionary in the face of our pointing out logical fallacies. Hence, their double pleasure.

5. Lastly here, but not finally, I find Pat's overall argument—which moves dialectically to a synthesis of what she refers to as a civil rhetoric—to be another one that is based on Cynicism as I've suggested throughout above. And, again, one in relation to this heuristic of noncontradiction for which she offers no reasons for its acceptance. This principle of formal, Parmenidean logic is the epitome of 'authority without truth' and with big or little 't.' Which is okay if we still-Moderns—and we are—mostly cynics! Remember as I opened these notes: ". . . we must make no mistake about ourselves: we are as much automaton as mind. . . . Proofs only convince the mind; habit provides the strongest proofs and those that are most believed. It inclines the automaton, which leads the mind unconsciously along with it." Habit leads Pat's mind to lead ours to habitually go with this principle of species-genus analytics, this dividing practice (diaeresis). So as to rule out contradictions. Žižek writes: "Pascal's [understanding], then, is: leave rational argumentation and submit yourself simply to ideological ritual, stupefy yourself by repeating the meaningless gestures [of accepting the principle of noncontradiction], act as if you already believe, and the belief will come by itself" (39). NONCONTRADICTION, the sublime Object will believe for us.

Week #11

Notes Used for 3 November 1998 Seminar Meeting. –vjv

A Major Interrogation of JB's Work (MAlcorn).

I have selected Marshall's article for several reasons:

> Alcorn, Marshall. "Changing the Subject of Postmodernist Theory: Discourse, Ideology, and Therapy in the Classroom." *Rhetoric Review* 13.2 (1995): 331–349.

I have selected Marshall's article for several reasons:

(1) It is the primary—if not the only direct—interrogation of JB's work on *praxis* (critical thinking and acting) in the classroom; (2) It is exceptionally clear and to the point, which can be heuristically made unclear in dis/order to remake clear in yet other ways and for yet other points; (3) It can help think another answer (which can proleptically present us with a fundamentally different Question) for Why JB's methodology may or can lead students but to cynicism (see Sloterdijk, *Critique of Cynical Reason*; Vitanza, "The Wasteland Grows," for *The Research Network Forum*, CCCC, 1998); (4) and most importantly, It may or can lead to ways of improving dialogically on JB's thinking about praxis.

The intention should be to problematize for the purpose of 'improving' on. (This is, after all, a dialectical process, but not leading to any Truth. I would prefer in my own way to say, 'These are—after all has been said and undone and redone for perpetual deterritorialization paralogoi or dissoi-paralogoi processes. Dialectics smacks of an over burdening (dominating to frustration) of our 'selphs' with rationality, whereas Dissoi-paralogi smack 'we-(always already potential)-hysterics' in the face so that 'we' might momentarily be aware of a condition of the Logos as not being able to resolve a problem through a rational investigation, but through the intervention of Kairos, but a Nietzschean (joyful-pessimistic, nonpositive-affirmative) Kairos, and not a Platonic, Aristotelian, or Heideggeran negative Kairos. In these smackings on the faceless, Change and Choice are willed by Kairos. The

Unhuman. (I have purposefully reversed the "smack" [slap] on the face by Kairos, bringing us not to reason and calmness, but their opposites. In a non-positive affirmative essentialism, I am saying, history is not always Human.) VVhich of course would drive JB—and did often—up the wall. (For a full very logical, yet perverse, explanation, via Untersteiner, see *Negation*. . . . [242–45].)

I would venture to say that Marshall's article, for me, may or can lead to ways of improving on the thought behind Freire's own notion of How language (logos) is a liberating force, is the source for the "ontological vocation," that is, the source for **Being calling us to freedom**. (I have made much of this Freirean notion, which is in line with the Isocratean and Freudian notions of the Logos. See previous weeks' class notes and my *Negation, Subjectivity, and The History of Rhetoric* 132, 364 [n.12].) In P. Friere's as well as in JB's notion of How the 'subject' (that-is-an-object) moves toward liberation, there is a (an innocent) belief in the beneficence of the Logos. Even in Catholicism, there is no such belief about the Logos. Or is there? I don't remember its Being-there, unless it's a romanticized Catholicism. If we take the Logos to be our Guide (*hegemoon*, Prince, Leader), then we will find ourselves forever in trouble. The common intention here in terms of the Guide is that it, she, he is beneficent. SING: "Someday, Our Princeeeeeee will comeeeeeee!!!" Feminists have given up on this topos; it's time for all of us to give it up! There is no Savior of humankind that is not also a destroyer. But there is a Kairos Beyond Good and Evil. But I digress. Or do I?

Let's turn more efficiently now to Marshall's discussion:

And let us Invent by way of Mourning and Melancholia, while Being-aware that this is a Modernist method of Invention! My thesis—or is it feces (see KB *GM*, 23)—is that I am against ('contra to,' yet 'alongside') Mourning as inventing the problem of JB's thinking. (I facilitated a graduate seminar on **Invention: classical, modern, and postmodern** in which we took up the issue and value[s] of Invention with Freud's 'mourning and melancholy' as well as 'paraphraxes.' Such methods are thoroughly Modernist!) And my question—or is it a quest?—is Whether Mourning becomes electr(icity). Neither of these of course is explained in any clear way, but they will do for what I desire to do. Here.

My expositions of Marshall's readings, therefore, are going to be skewed. This should be no problem since Marshall is here with us, though a problem (permanently) that JB is not. And yet, Is he not? but that's a Modernist invention of a question, right?

I want for the most part to skip over very quickly Marshall's exposition of JB's understanding of a postmodern subjectivity and focus instead on Marshall's interrogation and identification of a problem:

Marshall writes:

> Berlin believes that composition instruction should provide students with a greater control and understanding of the world of discourse that surrounds and constitutes them. This control is conceived of as a kind of cognitive power that students wrest from the more ubiquitous social and discursive power expressed through ideology....
>
> I largely support the postmodernist composition program Berlin advocates.... But because I agree with Berlin on so much, I feel it important to argue that the human subject is more complex than Berlin and others theorize. Postmodernist theory is still in a state of evolution, and its current account of the subject is, I think insufficiently complex for understanding relationships among language, subjectivity, and ideology.... If Berlin had allowed his description of classroom behavior to become more fully integrated with his theoretical claims, he might have been prompted to formulate a more Lacanian description of the subject that would lead, I believe, to more useful ideas both for negotiating the ideological conflicts generated in the classroom and for achieving the cognitive power that Berlin seeks. Lacan's subject is structured by a libidinal signification that it cannot easily bring into responsible self-awareness in the manner Berlin describes. (331–32)

We have dealt in seminar **(oops, another break . . .)**

With this incipient question of Why is it that JB backs off from dealing with the rich complexity that is in the theories (and in the 'reception histories' of those theories) he attempts to appropriate? To control!

(Recall JB's partial borrowings from Foucault when JB was doing revisionary historiography. Recall that he has read and cites Paul Smith [*Discerning the Subject*] but takes so selectively from him an impoverished notion of the subject [agent], which supposedly will not hamper or threaten the notion of social-epistemic rhetoric. . . . Later, I will talk about the use of partial theories—as in 'Travelling Theories' [E. Said]—and how what we suppress as what-we-do-not-want from those theories only comes back to

> (**A modernist reminiscence:** I remember once, now lost in time, that Jim attended an interdisciplinary conference that had Freire as the main speaker. Afterwards, Jim called and said, 'Victor, you would not believe this conference and what happened. There were all of these typical anti-theorists there attacking those of us who do theory. Finally, when it was time for Freire to speak and then to take questions, these anti-theorists started hailing an answer from him. "Freire—Oh, Master—are you not against unclear, theoretical, obscure prose?" ' Jim recounted that there was this long pause and Freire said, '"Thinking and writing are not like walking. Thinking and writing are very difficult." ')

haunt us. Readers who read and express little value for fearing theory will, nonetheless, bring these excluded sections of, say, Foucault right back while reading JB's accounts. Then what?)

We have pointed to the problems of audience. Jim wanted to reach for and to have an impact on teachers of writing who might be turned off by discussions of theory. This is all too humanly, human, all too understandable but all too counterproductive in the long run. After all, there is that audience of theorists that reads JB's works as well. As a case in point: Marshall puts his finger right on the 'Invention(s) of Clarity' when he writes: "In seeking simple and useful clarity, Berlin makes clearly visible the contradictions in the various modules of postmodernist theory he has spliced together to fashion a persuasive pedagogy" (334). "Clarity"—the element of Clarity—is a very unstable one, breaking down and opening itself to radical multiplicities. Clarity is quite inventive, no? In its perversity. But What about (again) the principle of (Invention by way of) Contradiction(s)?, which I discussed in dis/respect to Pat Bizzell's location of contradictions in JB's MLA paper. I would agree here that Contradictions can be inventive, but must not necessarily be corrected, as I would agree that misspellings can be inventive (as in 'paraphraxes'), but must not necessarily be corrected. To put it more bluntly: Jim was not expressing a *contradiction*; he was expressing *mixed feelings,* ambivalences, etc.

Mourning and Melancholia are not Contradictions. To call them such would be applying two different universes of discourse that might—and often do—create a differend (Lyotard). Which we could use, as we will, I hope, quite effectively to rethink JB's ambivalences. Polylogoi.

Let us return to Marshall, who writes:

> Berlin makes two claims about ideology. First, he describes what ideology offers a culture. It offers a vision of what is 'necessary, normal or inevitable.' [from Goran Therborn] Ideology confines a culture within a restricted horizon of imagination. Second, however, Berlin observes that ideology does not function simply at the level of human imagination. It is allied with various subtle and not so subtle policing forces. Ideology 'brings with it strong social and cultural enforcement.
>
> This observation about the external enforcement of ideology is important because Berlin, like most postmodernists, argues that it is ideology—and not some putative structure 'within' subjectivity—that provides stability to the subject. . . . Subjectivity is by nature a structure multiple, conflicted, and unpredictable; ideology intervenes in this structure to give it pattern and definition.
>
> Effective composition instruction, Berlin argues, will clarify and resist the policing action of ideology. 'We must take as our province,' he says, 'the production and reception of semiotic

codes broadly conceived, providing students with **the heuristics to penetrate these codes and their ideological designs** on our formation as the subjects of our experience.' Given this objective of penetrating ideological codes, however, one must ask how it is done. How is the subject, who is a subject precisely because she has been interpellated by the discourse of ideology, able to overcome ideological victimization? Put simply, how does the subject, as one ideological composition, become another ideological composition?" (332–33; emphasis added)

A good question(s)! And yes, Marshall, the word 'penetration' is unstable while it speaks of the power of **the phallus**. JB speaks much of the power to CONTROL (discipline) oneself or Others. By(e) way of Rationality!

After interrogating this word, this heuristic in terms of How? and What? Marshall asks, "If Berlin has chosen his words carefully, we should ask how eros and/or hostility serve in the unmasking of ideology he advocates" (333).

Marshall now takes a close look at how Berlin repeatedly describes his classroom in democratic terms: "Berlin describes himself operating within an environment of democratic principles. 'The social-epistemic classroom,' he says, 'offers a lesson in democracy, intended to prepare students for critical participation in public life'" (333). Marshall points out: "Lessons in democracy imply principles of rationality, choice, and recognition of self-interest, no coercion, programming, intimidation, or seduction. Democracies assume, in principle at least, that citizens, given knowledge and the freedom to act, will act in their own best interests" (333).

Ah, the Contras' Diction: That, in Spite, Invents? Ah, Contras' Diction: That in Spite, Invents?

Marshall describes Berlin as expressing "very traditional liberal ideals" (334). And then he asks the big question: "**Why does Berlin describe a *constructed* subject in theory, but a *free* subject in classroom practice?**" (334; emphasis added).

In a lengthy discussion of Althusser's theory of the subject and in an excellent analogy between teachers 'shouting lessons' and Orwell's account of "how antifascist soldiers on the front lines in the Spanish Civil War were given not only combat duty but also what was termed 'shouting duty'" (as in interpellations of students and soldiers to duty), Marshall shows and argues,

> "Human subjects, while they do show multiple and conflicting identities, also **reveal defensive resistances to discourse manipulation**. If you 'fill' a person's mind with new

discourse, there is little chance this person will 'be' this new discourse. Real-world experience suggests that something apparently 'within' a subject mediates between discourse 'characteristic' of a particular subject and discourse that seeks to change a subject's identity. Something within a subject operates to preserve and maintain a characteristic identity. [An anti-political theory of stasis!] This mechanism . . . prompts subjects to actively process rather than passively internalize the discourse they are given. Because of a kind of adhesive 'attachment' [libidinal attachment] that subjects have to certain instances of discourse, some discourse structures are 'characteristic' of subjects and have a temporal stability. These modes of discourse serve as 'symptoms' of subjectivity: they work repeatedly and defensively to represent identity.

Lacanian theory suggests that subjects, in their adhesive attachment to discourse, defend and tenaciously repeat the 'symptoms' of their subjectivity. Lacan's description of subjectivity as a form of defense should lead us to more fully appreciate the problems of 'penetrating' or undoing the libidinal attachments subjects have to discourse. Lacan's theory of the subject, like Althusser's, suggests that subjectivity is not, as Berlin suggests, an **amoebae** eagerly absorbing all the discourse that it encounters. It is more like an **insect** with a hard outer skeletal system that protects its inner structure from penetration—from the hostilely invasive facts and discourse that threaten its image of contained and harmonious self-identity

Berlin evades this question: How does the subject rebel against the ideological discourse that defensively maintains its own subjectivity? The work of Lacan and Althusser, reflecting the evidence of everyday experience, suggests that **many subjects would prefer to be biologically dead** [wwwwwwhat! Ahhhhhhhaaaaaaaaaaaaa! How(l), did this statement make it into the post-Berlin era of publishing this ms.? Is this a symptom of our loss and rationalization to give JB a good critical fun e rail?] than to exist as different subjects of discourse. This recognition should have sobering effects on teachers who believe that a simple, clear, and rational explanation of political activity can directly lead to different political identifications. Too often these explanations fail to work precisely because they function not as explanations but as **threats to the life principle of the subject** [wwwwwwwhat!? Ahhhhhhhhhhhhh!]." (338–39; emphasis very much mine)

This (C. Auguste Dupin prose) all explains more than I want to know, given the circumstances of our Being-here!

The In(ter)ventional Moment: Contra Dictions Talk to Us

Which leads us to ourselves. Marshall writes: "Berlin claims to understand the subject's constructed nature and its inability to be rational and free, but he advocates a pedagogy that is absolutely dependent upon the subject's *ability* to be rational and free. . . . If we believe these cliams, we must rethink Berlin's theoretical account of a postmodernist pedagogy" (339).

A fix in terms of ... three models

> **First ("postmodern") Model:** . . . "the one that Berlin appeals to in his description of classroom practice . . . is an awkward synthesis of humanist and postmodernist beliefs. In the classroom Berlin assumes that because the subject is a structure of ideology conflict, this conflict can lead naturally to a kind of resolution through knowledge and political action. Berlin's theoretical description, however, contradicts this model of resolution. There is nothing in Berlin's post-modern theory to suggest that any resolution of conflict is possible. The postmodernist subject, unlike the humanist subject, is *essentially* a structure of discourse conflict; it has no mechanism or motivation for being anything *other* than such a structure of conflict. A teacher could never hope to change the structure of, or resolve the conflict in, a subject by merely adding more discourse or more conflict to the subject" (339–40).

> **Second ("structuralist") Model "pushed by discourse":** The "idea of subjects becoming transformed through external discourse is the second model to which Berlin appeals when describing the possibility for political change in the classroom. In this essentially structuralist model, change occurs not from within subjectivity but through the discourse dynamics operating in the classroom. In this model the subject never has freedom, never 'chooses' anything" . . . is, instead, a mere effect of language (340–41).

> **Third ("psychoanalytic") Model:** "This model . . . suggests that discourse or language is, in itself, a highly heterogeneous substance. On the one hand, it *can* operate as coded information, able to influence political identity largely in terms of the old liberal categories of knowledge and truth. On the other hand, discourse can act as a highly libidinal substance. It is the material embodiment of human emotion, of emotionally charged thinking, and emotionally intense identification. This libidinal language is in fact the material instrument of subjective 'penetration: [sic.] 'seductive' rhetoric, invasive fantasy, and hostile assertion. . . . A cogent postmodernist and cultural pedagogy requires an understanding not simply of ideology but of the libidinal power of ideological language. The libidinal power of language is found in its potential for attachments, attractions, organizations, repulsions, and bindings that create relatively stable sites of identification and disidentification wherein particular subjects locate themselves in a particularized language. Libidinal language refers in part to bodily experiences (often sensed as emotion) that signal the libidinal attachments that humans have to objects and ideas represented by language. To be attentive to libidinal language, we must develop a pattern of attentiveness somewhat different from the one we use in considering the meaning of ideological language.
>
> The push of libidinal language involves a pressure and rhetorical interplay of emotion. . . . To be clear and consistent, rational and 'penetrating' about the claims that subjects are pushed by language, we need a theory of libidinal pusing to complicate a theory of ideology. . . . But this libidinal force . . . is also irrational, often unconscious, and generally resistant to conscious intervention and control. Berlin describes ideological conflict as if it were a linguistic code a subject could logically read and rewrite. He wants to be rational and to appeal to both subject's ability to recognize conflictual codings and be free from bad conflict. . ." (341).
>
> "Reducing unconscious conflict, Lacanian theory shows, is not a simple matter accomplished efficiently and effectively by rational and informative speech. Saying to a person, 'Look at these conflicting codes; you have unconscious conflict here,' does not make the person recognize and resolve such conflict. This process of recognition . . . is made difficult because it is charged with all the processes of erotics, aggression, displacement, and defense . . . that subjects exhibit in maintaining their identities" (343).

It is this third model, of course, that Marshall proposes as a means of rethinking the problematic that JB is not only **in** but also that JB **is**.

A Grave Message: That Fails? Yet DIEalectically deSynthesizes ...

The third section of the article (not unlike Bizzell's third section . . . See Week 10. . . . Thirds are not representable! . . . "My original essay," Marshall rebegins, "had another ending. In my earlier draft, I ended by emphasizing the differences between libidinal language and rational language. Rather than include my original concluding section here, however, I have decided to try to publish it later [as it is now published at the Berlin site and will have been published in *PRE/TEXT* PULP.] I will end this present essay on a more personal note—(following one reviewer's suggestion)—with more generalized reflections . . ." (343). It is extremely difficult to read this third section without hearing the libidinal attachments announcing themselves. I cannot say ironies. But 'libidinal attachments.'

> "But how are we to take this 'letter' here? Quite simply, literally." –J. Lacan, "The Agency of the Letter in the Unconscious ,or Reason since Freud" in *Ecrit*.

JB is quoted by Marshall as saying in his letter to Thea Enos: "I have been reading in the very Lacanian materials the author [MAlcorn] mentions in the essay in preparation for a book titled A Teacher's Guide [hegemon, prince, leader, guide!] *to Cultural Studies*" (344).

Marshall writes: "Berlin had hoped, when this essay was published, to publish a short reply. " 'Should my essay be published [buried, as the original ending was, and yet irrepressibly returned] alongside hers?' he wrote to Enos. 'When do you need my response? (Since I feel a lot is at stake here, I can safely promise that I will be right on time with my essay.' Berlin, however, could not be on time with his response. He died about a month after he wrote his letter [his letter to ?] Enos, and his reply to this essay will not be forthcoming.

And yet, because of Berlin's extended letter, I can quote from some of the reactions. Berlin was uneasy with the emphasis that I was giving to personal experience:

> 'I want to keep a good discussion on track, one that this author goes a long way toward starting. I also want to address some small disagreements, such as the distinction made between the central place of ideology in abstract politics and the lack of ideology in the libidinal attachments of the subject. . . This disagreement is important since the wrong take on it can lead **the expressivists** in the audience to once again abandon the political and public in favor of the libidinal and private. This has already appeared in certain commentators on poststructuralist theory who call upon the challenge to foundations and the split subject to argue for a revival of Peter Elbow and the celebration of the personal.'" (344)

The libidinal is private? is like saying/asking The political is private? The libidinal is public; the public (body) is composed of and by the libidinal. Therein lies . . . lies in an extra-moral sense . . . the difference.

What lingers, haunts, the text of JB is **the expressivist**. The libidinal attachment to or with the expressivist. The eternal return of the expressivist! Marshall writes in his second, published ending: "I will end this present essay on a more personal note—(following one reviewer's suggestion)—with more generalized reflections upon the issues I have raised" (343). Xpressivism returns to haunt the letter that JB sent, as the repressed letter that returns haunts bye way of expressiveness. Though die a logically!

> The whole last section, rewritten for publication in *RR*, is epiedictic. Is an **expression** of knowing that while "a person we know is dead, we cannot simply abandon our libidinal attachments" that invent his return. "Mourning shows the extent to which we will all insist upon having that which we cannot have even when we know that our desire for an object is futile or irrational" (346).

Marshall concludes, rebegins: "If ideologies are bad, they are bad not because some authority says so, but because they make us, or people we care for, suffer. But this precisely is the problem. Subjects would often rather suffer from a bad ideology [or die] than suffer from changing their ideology. Ideology can [be] the bad mother [M Alcorn] who is better than no mother. . . . Our most common response to those who try to push us toward mourning is anger and hatred, the gestures of the countertransference. And yet this change we resist may be what we most need" (348).

Weeks #12-13

Notes UnUseable for 10,17 November 1998 Seminar Meetings. –vjv

The Final Book, Published Posthumously

Whether I will be the hero of my story or the villain, "I" do not know.' In response to this allusion, I would assert that in Jim's autobiography (his last strong will and testament), he is the hero of our story:

> Berlin, James A. **Rhetorics, Poetics, and Cultures: Refiguring College English Studies**. Urbana, Illinois: NCTE, 1996. Rpt with a new foreword and response essays by Parlor Press, 2004.

Don't get me wrong/ful! There's much that I find lacking in the story, but those (my) findings are neither here nor there. It's his story cum ours and he gets to de**term**ine it as he wishes with the help of all those who wrote this book of experiences with him. We all did, and especially those of his graduate students and his mentors, referred to in the second half of the book. But Jim, himself, struggles with and en/joys writing this book.

I said, essentially, what I wanted to say at the CCCC in Chicago on the panel with Janice Lauer, Linda Brodkey, Lester Faigley, John Trimbur, Patricia Harkin, and Susan Miller. (Cool People! 'Twas an honor to have been with them and us.) These sayings were published in **JAC**.

More to the point: I don't think that I need or even desire to respond to this book here, at this point in time. I do have much, far too much to say and in great detail, step by step, . . . [in respect to the middle part, where Jim responds to me] . . . but it (all) 'finally' seems not necessary as well as inappropriate. InApProPoMo. If YoU cAtCh My DrIfT!

I will return to this one-cum-many books, if *time* and *opportunity* (chance occurrences and gifts [Kairos/oi]) allow me. They always have; and they always almost will have. ;-)

Weeks #14-15

Notes for 24 November, 1 December 1998 Seminar Meetings. —vjv

The Retrospective

You or we might re/begin with the assumption, or predisposition, that JB's work is done and therefore we will (be about) looking back. If so, we would be wrong/ful.

> Berlin, James A. **All and still more of 'Our' Work!**. Everywhere: University and Independent Presses, 2XXX.

JB's work is done in one sense, but a rather impoverished sense of thinking about someone's work; his work is not done in another sense, a rather productive (interventional, heuristic) sense of thinking about some many works. JB is many. Is this not what JB meant in terms of social-epistemic. (The 'revolution' is never over but perpetually worked towards by us.) We must understand this approach to thinking about his and others' works.

The task before us is ripe with difficulty. I have stated in our preparations for this Retrospective that we stress the affirmative. All in the affirmative.

The Field: Therefore, I would begin by repeating what I said in the seminar description and then locate a few additional re/descriptions:

To study the works of Berlin is to study the field of composition from the mid-1980s to the present day.

Berlin's Topologies thoroughly and perpetually re-mapped the field and therefore determined what could be said and not said about composition theories and pedagogies; what could be thought about textbooks in the field and what could not be thought; what could be seen as ethically and politically acceptable reasons for teaching literacy and what could not."

I still maintain this to be true (though I am well aware that there is no "The Field," but fields and other things). We can certainly point to others who have mapped the field such as James Kinneavy, and we have during the first week. Many come before us. But none other than Jim so plotted the field politically and ethically as he has. So emplotted, it ideologically, in order to say that the noetic fields within the discipline are ideological. There is no saying or making or doing that is not ideological (unless, of course, we begin to talk about 'surfaces' in the sense that Baudrillard does, but we will not to talk about that now). In identifying the fields as ideological, JB made them once ever again ideological. THE DISCIPLINE ACCORDING TO JB! We all do make it "According to us" in our various ways, though "WE" do so together. Socially. (There is no "personal" ideology, I would still maintain. Expressivism may be 'personal,' but always already 'social,' as I take JB as saying. It just happens to be that particular brands of the personal are not socially acceptable, as I take Jim to be saying.)

Map/s: JB created, it follows from the above and I repeat, the map/s of the new discipline. Students who would enter the field would do themselves well to begin with JB's work, and then to think by/e way of it.

Audience: JB respected and wrote for all of us, but none more important/ly than for "teachers of writing." I have often wondered, What if he had written solely for a company of theorists, What would he have said then? But no matter, now. JB was writing for the right audience. Given what he had to say and given how he cared for the discipline, JB could not not write for any other audience than "teachers of writing." This audience is real, good, and though impossible at time, this audience/s is/are nonetheless THE audience/s of possibilities. We must embrace the challenge as JB did from the beginning.

Travelling Theories: JB, like any bricoleur, borrowed what was ready-at-hand, and built theories and praxies with his borrowings. But what is especially important to understand is that he borrowed parts of this person's theory and the next person's theory. He borrowed, which we all do, what suits "our" interests. His borrowings, however, were, for me, bothersome, for he would take parts as if they could be de/parted from what he left behind. I have criticized him for such borrowings, such as his takings from Foucault (see, e.g., class notes for week 6. The affirmative side of my criticism of his borrowings is that JB allows us to see, as never before, how excluded borrowings refuse to remain excluded. How they return. Forever. (This refusal is real, good, and only possible while, from a Modernist point of view, it's 'the impossible'—that is to say, out of the impossible comes the possible. It's the old type view of pre/Modernist Inventional procedures: Out of Nothing [the negative, or absence of the real] comes everything.)

Standing His Ground: JB stood firm with his beliefs. His political interests, no matter what. This is to be admired, only admired, for under fire or deep criticism, most people turn. And run. He could take criticism. He learned from it. Instead of always un/just deflecting it. In Order to survive. He THRIVED on it. Both Hissed *at* and Laughed *with* it.

Critique: There's an older, by now, saying: "We want Democratic Socialism—we want the Revolution to be successful—so that we can critique it." What is wonderful is that Jim gave us a beginning revolution to critique, to improve on. We did so critique it when he was alive and we will have critiqued it while he is yet still alive in "our" sayings, doings, makings. This is how(l) we all will have lived on and on and on, etc.

Some More: As I hinted at in the last double weeks' class notes, there is always more to say. And That VVill Have Been Said.

So please return here.

From time to time.

On y/our way to the Revolution or Wherevers!

Appendices

W o r k s (selections)

Books

Writing Instruction in Nineteenth-Century American Colleges. Carbondale: SIUP, 1984.

Rhetoric and Reality: Writing Instruction in American Colleges. 1900–1985. Carbondale: SIUP, 1987.

Rhetorics, Poetics, and Cultures: Refiguring College English Studies. Parlor Press. 2003. (Afterword by Janice M. Lauer. Response essays by Linda Brodkey, Patricia Harkin, Susan Miller, John Trimbur, and Victor J. Vitanza).

Inventing a Discipline: Rhetoric Scholarship in Honor of Richard E. Young. Ed. Maureen Daly Goggin. National Council of Teachers of English, 2000. (Foreword by Richard Leo Enos. Essays by Charles Bazerman, Maureen Daly Goggin and Steve Beatty, Janice M. Lauer, Joseph Petraglia, Robert Inkster, Eugene Garver, Karen Rossi Schnakenbergy, Winifred Bryan Horner, Victor J. Vitanza ["From Heuristic to Aleatory Procedures; or, Toward Writing the Accident"], Lee Odell and Karen McGrane, Danette Paul and Ann M. Blakeslee, Carol Berlenkotter, Elenore Long, Sam Watson, Stuart Greene and Rebecca Schoenike Nowacek, Mike Palmquiste, Jo-Ann M. Sipple, William L. Sipple, and J. Stanton Carson.)

Articles in Journals and Chapters in Books

"Composition Studies and Cultural Studies: Collapsing Boundaries." *Into the Field: Sites of Composition Studies.* Ed. Anne Ruggles Gere. NY: MLA, 1993. 99–116.

"Composition and Cultural Studies." *Composition and Resistance.* Eds. Hurlbert, C. Mark and Michael Blitz. Portsmouth, NH: Boynton/Cook, 1991.

"Contemporary Composition: The Major Pedagogical Theories." *College English* 44 (1982): 765–777.

"Cultural Studies." *Encyclopedia of Rhetoric and Composition.* Ed. Theresa Enos. NY: Garland, 1996. 154–56.

"Freirean Pedagogy in the U.S.: A Response." *JAC* 12 (Fall 1992): 414–21.

"James Berlin Responds. 'Rhetoric and Ideology in the Writing Class.'" *College English* 51 (1989): 770–77.

"Postmodernism, Politics, and Histories of Rhetorics." *PRE/TEXT* 11.3–4 (1990): 169–87.

"Poststructuralism, Cultural Studies, and the Composition Classroom." *Rhetoric Review* 11 (Fall 1992): 16–33. Rpt. *Professing the New Rhetoric*. Ed. Theresa Enos and Stuart C. Brown. Englewood Cliffs, New Jersey: Prentice Hall, 1994. 461–80.

"Postmodernism, the College Curriculum, and Composition." *Composition in Context. Essays in Honor of Donald C. Stewart*. Ed. W. Ross Winterowd and Vincent Gillespie. Carbondale, Illinois: SIUP, 1994. 46–61.

"Revisionary History: The Dialectical Method." *PRE/TEXT* 8.1–2 (1987): 47–61.

"Revisionary Histories of Rhetoric: Politics, Power, and Plurality." *Writing Histories of Rhetoric*. Ed. Victor J. Vitanza. Carbondale: SIUP, 1994. 112–27.

"Rhetoric and Ideology in the Writing Class." *College English* 50 (1988): 477–94.

"Rhetoric and Poetics in the English Department: Our Nineteenth-Century Inheritance." *College English* 47 (1985): 531–33.

"Richard Whately and Current-Traditional Rhetoric." *College English* 42 (September 1980): 10–17.

"A Prospective." *PRE/TEXT: The First Decade*. Ed. Victor J. Vitanza. Pittsburgh Series in Composition, Literacy, and Culture. Pittsburgh: U of Pittsburgh P, 1993.

"Rhetoric, Poetic, and Culture: Contested Boundaries in English Studies." *The Politics of Writing Instruction: Postsecondary*. Ed. Richard Bullock and John Trimbur. Portmouth, NH: Boynton Cook Heinemann, 1991, 23–38.

"Foreword." *Changing Classroom Practices: Resources for Literary and Cultural Studies*. Ed. David Downing. Urbana, IL: NCTE, 1994. vii-xii.

•

Berlin, James A., and Robert P. Inkster. "Current-Traditional Rhetoric: Paradigm and Practice." *Freshman English News* 8. 3 (Winter 1980): 1–4, 13–14.

Berlin, James A., et al. Octalog. "The Politics of Historiography." *Rhetoric Review* 7 (1988): 5–49.

Interviews

Connery, Brian A., and Van E. Hillard, "Dialectical Notions: An Interview with Jim Berlin." *Writing on the Edge*. 3.2 (1992).

McDonald, Robert L., and James Berlin, "An Interview with James Berlin." *Composition Studies*, Vol. 22, No. 1 (Spring 1994), pp. 25–43.

Major Edited Works

Berlin, James A., and Michael Vivion, eds. *Cultural Studies in the English Classroom*. Portsmouth, NH: Boynton, Cook, Heinman Portsmouth, 1992.

Berlin, James A., and John Trimbur, Guest Editors. Special Issue: "Marxism and Rhetoric." *PRE/TEXT* 13. 1–2. (1992).

Major Secondary Material (directed toward Berlin)

Alcorn, Marshall. "Changing the Subject of Postmodernist Theory: Discourse, Ideology, and Therapy in the Classroom." *Rhetoric Review* 13.2 (1995): 331–349.

Bizzell, Patricia. "Beyond anti-Foundationalism Rhetorical Authority: Problems Defining 'Cultural Literacy.'" *College English* 52.6 (1990): 661–675. (Critique of Berlin on pp. 670, 672–73)

Connors, Robert J. Rev. of *Writing Instruction in Nineteenth-Century American Colleges*, James A. Berlin. *College Composition and Communications* 37 (1986): 247–49.

Crowley, Sharon. Rev of *Rhetoric and Reality: Writing Instruction in American Colleges: 1900–1985*, James A. Berlin. *College Composition and Communications* 39 (1986): 245–47.

Downing, David B., James J. Sosnoski, with Keith Dorwick, eds. *Cultural Studies and Composition: Conversations in Honor of James Berlin*. *Works and Days* 14.1–2 (1996).

Faigley, Lester. *Fragments of Rationality: Postmodernity an the Subject of Composition*. Pittsburgh: U of Pittsburgh P, 1992.

Flower, Linda. "Comments on James Berlin. 'Rhetoric and Ideology in the Writing Class.'" *College English* 51 (1989): 765–69.

Jim Berlin's Last Work: Future Perfect, Tense (A collection of articles by Linda Brodkey, Patricia Harkin, Susan Miller, John Trimbur, and Victor J. Vitanza on Rhetorics, Poetics, Cultures). *JAC* 17.3 (1997): 489–505.

Schilb, John. "Comments on James Berlin. 'Rhetoric and Ideology in the Writing Class.'" *College English* 51 (1989): 769–70.

Scriben, Karen. "Comments on James Berlin. 'Rhetoric and Ideology in the Writing Class.'" *College English* 51 (1989): 764–65.

Major Secondary Material (used by Berlin)

Fogarty, Daniel. *Roots for a New Rhetoric*. NY: Teachers College, Columbia U, 1959.

Freire, Paulo. *Pedagogy of the Oppressed*. NY: Continuum, 1970.

Kitzhaber, Albert R. "Rhetoric in American Colleges, 1850–1900." Diss. Washington U, 1953; in published form, *Rhetoric in American Colleges*, 1850–1900. Dallas, TX: Southern Methodist UP, 1990.

Ohmann, Richard. *English in America: A Radical View of the Profession*. NY: Oxford UP, 1976.

Shor, Ira. *Critical Teaching and Everyday Life*. Chicago: U of Chicago, 1987.

Therborn, Goran. *The Ideology of Power and the Power of Ideology*. London: Verso, 1980.

Williams, Raymond. *Keywords: A Vocabulary of Culture and Society*. Revised Edition. NY: Oxford UP, 1977.

Last modified July 5, 1998 // Last modified March 12, 2011 // April 25, 2020

NEH Seminar

Berlin participated in a 9-month seminar during the 1978–1979 academic year. The Topic of the Seminar was "Rhetorical Invention and the Composing Process." The seminar was composed of ten Fellows: Sharon Bassett, James A. Berlin, Lisa Ede, David Fractenberg, Robert P. Inkster, Charles Kneupper, Victor J. Vitanza, Sam Watson, Jr., Vickie Winkler, and William Nelson. The seminar Leader was Richard E. Young (Carnegie-Mellon University, Pittsburgh).

A Personal Note: Rummaging Around in my Notes taken during the Seminar—vjv:

I have a large box filled with my notes, handouts, articles from the seminar and letters exchanged after the seminar. Below are some bits of information that might be of some value to someone.

Speakers/Visitors to the Seminar

> Linda Flower (who was teaching writing in the Business College, CMU, at the time)
> Richard Ohmann,
> Pete Becker (. . .of Young, Becker, and Pike)
> Bill Coles (U of Pittsburgh)
> A. D. Van Nostrand (Brown U)
> Richard Enos (who was interviewed for a position at CMU)
> Otis M. Walter (U of Pittsburgh, Speech)
> Janice Lauer (U of Detroit)
> Henry Johnstone (A group of the Fellows drove to Penn St. and visited with Johnstone and others involved in editing Philosophy and Rhetoric.)

Linda Flower and Dick Hayes, Protocols

About seven of the Fellows gave two protocols each so that F/H could do their early research on the composing process. Their publications refer to their so-called "expert" writers. Jim Berlin gave two protocols.

Conferences Attended and Participated In

College Composition and Communication, Minneapolis, April 5–7, 1979.
Conference on English Education, Pittsburgh, March 16–18, 1979.
Popular Culture, Pittsburgh, April 1979.
Learning to Write (Canadian Council of Teachers of English), Ottawa, May 8–14, 1979.

Dissertations Included on Seminar Reading List

Albert Raymond Kitzhaber, Janice Lauer, Hal Rivers Weidner.

There were additional dissertations that Young had in his office, which he suggested to individuals in the seminar, most of which were on Tagmemics and done by linguists.

For published discussions of the seminar, see:

A retrospective and prospective explaining how the journal *PRE/TEXT* grew out of the experience of the seminar:

Vitanza, Victor J. "A Retrospective."
Berlin, James A. "A Prospective."

In *PRE/TEXT: The First Decade*. Ed. Victor J. Vitanza. Pittsburgh Series in Composition, Literacy, and Culture. Pittsburgh, The U of Pittsburgh P, 1993.

A dissertation on the seminar: (The pdf is on line. Use the name and title.)

ACCESSION NO.: AAI9513235
TITLE: AN NEH FELLOWSHIP EXAMINED: SOCIAL NETWORKS AND COMPOSITION HISTORY
AUTHOR: ALMAGNO, STEPHANIE A.
DEGREE: PH.D.
YEAR: 1994
INSTITUTION: UNIVERSITY OF RHODE ISLAND; 0186
SOURCE: DAI, VOL. 55-12A, Page 3765, 00141 Pages
DESCRIPTORS: EDUCATION, HISTORY OF; EDUCATION, LANGUAGE AND LITERATURE

ABSTRACT:

Until now, histories of composition studies have been predicated on the idea that discipline formation stems solely from textual evidence generated by individual scholars; few histories, however, take account the influence of social networks formed by the field's professionals. Addressing what Janice Lauer refers to as "loopholes" in composition history, this dissertation constructs a working definition of social networks while it also offers an extended example of their historical significance. I focus on the 1978–79 NEH Fellowship, "Rhetorical Invention and the Composing Process," directed by Richard Young at Carnegie-Mellon University. From oral and print sources including interviews with or texts written by the fellowship participants, I gathered information concerning the social network that developed from the 1978–79 fellowship. I present this history of the fellowship as a conversation among the participants and the director. In addition, a section of commentary following the conversation indicates social networks' integral position in composition studies. In composition history, a discussion of discipline development is always complicated by its seemingly dissonant components which include journal formation, professional projects, conference presentations, and the role of networking among the field's professionals. A history of the field based on social networks, however, gathers these components and addresses them in relation to professional activity. This dissertation proposes a new way to examine traditional areas of inquiry within composition history.

Selected Citations on "Rhetoric as Epistemic" as Developed in Speech-Communication/Communication Studies.

* * *

(Please note that the phrase "rhetoric as epistemic" has a very rich tradition in Speech-Communication [Communication Studies] prior to Berlin's discussion of "social-epistemic rhetoric." Berlin draws initially on Robert Scott's discussion*, as well as on others'; then he takes the discussions to the important point of 'a socialist turn.')

* * *

Brummett, Barry. "The Reported Demise of Epistemic Rhetoric: A Eulogy for Epistemic Rhetoric." *The Quarterly Journal of Speech* 76 (Feb. 1990): 69–72.

—. "Some Implications of 'Process' or 'Intersubjectivity' Postmodern Rhetoric." *Philosophy and Rhetoric* 9 (1976): 21–51.

Cherwitz, Robert A. "Rhetoric as 'A Way of Knowing': An Attenuation of the Epistemological Claims of the 'New Rhetoric.'" *Southern Speech Communication Journal* 42 (Spring 1997): 207–19.

—. "Rhetoric as Epistemic: A Conversation with Richard A. Cherwitz" (conducted by Charles Kneupper). *PRE/TEXT* 5:3–4 (1984): 197–235.

Cherwitz, Robert A. and Hikins, James W. "Burying the Undertaker: A Eulogy for the Eulogists of Rhetorical Epistemology." *The Quarterly Journal of Speech* 76 (Feb. 1990): 73–77.

—. *Communication and Knowledge.* Columbia, SC: U of South Cariolina P, 1985.

—. "Toward a Rhetorical Epistemology." *SSCJ* 47 (Winter 1982): 135–62.

—. "Why the Epistemic in Epistemic Rhetoric? The Paradox of Rhetoric as Performance." *Text and Performance Quarterly* 15 (1995): 189–205.

Croasman, Earl, and Richard A. Cherwitz. "Beyond Rhetorical Relativism." *QJS* 68 (February 1982): 1–16.

Farrell, Thomas B. "From the Parthenon to the Bassinet: Death and Rebirth Along the Epistemic Trail." *The Quarterly Journal of Speech* 6 (Feb. 1990): 78–84.

Leff, Michael C. "In Search of Ariadne's Thread: A Review of the Recent Literature on Rhetorical Theory." *CSSJ* 29 (Summer 1978): 73–91. (An excellent summary and review of the work on Rhetoric as Epistemic up to 1978.)

Schroeder, John. "On Rhetoric-as-Epistemic: Has the Discussion Died?" http://www.niu.edu/acad/english/wac/schrepis.html.

*Scott, Robert L. "On Viewing Rhetoric as Epistemic." *Central States Speech Journal* 18 (1967): 9–16.

—. "On Viewing Rhetoric as Epistemic: Ten Years Later." *Central States Speech Journal* 27 (1976): 258–66.

—. "Epistemic Rhetoric and Criticism: Where Barry Brummett Goes Wrong." *The Quarterly Journal of Speech* 76 (1990): 300–03.

—. "Rhetoric as Epistemic: What Difference Does That Make?" *Defining the New Rhetorics.* Ed. Theresa Enos and Stuart C. Brown. Englewood Cliffs, New Jersey: Prentice Hall, 1994. 120–36.

* * *

Berlin's major Topologies in chronological order:

(Caveat: These topologies are basically categories or maps to think about discourse. The discussions that they enable are by far more important and valuable than the categories themselves. Knowing them, therefore, is of less value than knowing how to use them as a means of establishing tactics and strategies to think about discourse in writing instruction. Hence, they are listed here only as a quick reference, and they are by no means complete. We will study how JB used them—heuristically—for ethical-political ends.)

Berlin, James A., and Robert P. Inkster. "Current-Traditional Rhetoric: Paradigm and Practice." *Freshman English News* 8. 3 (Winter 1980): 1–4, 13–14.

Berlin and Inkster analyze four popular textbooks semiotically across the communications triangle of encoder (writer), decoder (reader), reality, and code (language) and conclude that the texts are based primarily on an epistemological view of reality as non-problematic and of language as a mere tool to describe reality. In their own words they warn that "the current-traditional paradigm is even more powerfully and profoundly entrenched than has been supposed" and "represents a danger to teachers, students, the wider purposes of our educational enterprise, and even our social and human fabric" (13).

"Contemporary Composition: The Major Pedagogical Theories." *College English* 44 (1982): 765-77.

- the Neo-Aristotelians or Classicists [reality can be known through sense experience],
- the Positivists or Current-Traditionalists [common-sense reality is determine inductively],
- the Neo-Platonists or Expressionists [reality is only appearance, but "truth" can be known through a "private vision" that is "inexpressible"], and
- the New Rhetoricians, or Social-Epistemic [the realities of the material world are socially constructed]. (766)
- *Writing Instruction in Nineteenth-Century American Colleges*. Carbondale: Southern Illinois UP, 1984.
- Classical (from Aristotle and others),
- Psychological-Epistemological (from 18th-century rhetoric),
- Romantic (from the American Transcendental movement).
- *Rhetoric and Reality: Writing Instruction in American Colleges. 1900–1985*. Carbondale: Southern Illinois UP, 1987.
- Objective Theories (CTR, behaviorist, semanticist, and linguistic rhetorics)
- Subjective Theories (romantic and liberal rhetorics; American Freudian and post-Freudian psychologies, with non-directive therapists)
- Transactional Theories (classical, cognitive, and epistemic) "Rhetoric and Ideology in the Writing Class." *College English* 50 (1988): 477–494.
- "cognitive rhetoric" (480–84) and "expressionistic rhetoric" (384–87).
- "*social-epistemic rhetoric*" (488–93).

* * *

Week #11: Supplement to the Readings and the Notes. –vjv

A Major Interrogation of JB's Work. (This is a link off of the class notes for Week #11.)

Below is the e-mail exchange between Marshall Alcorn me, and a copy of the original ending to Marshall's article on JB in ***Rhetoric Review***. What you find below was originally Section III, where the rewrite now begins on p. 343 of the article in print. I will eventually set up a Hyper News site for discussing the issues raised in both versions of the conclusion.

Alcorn, Marshall. "Changing the Subject of Postmodernist Theory: Discourse, Ideology, and Therapy in the Classroom." **Rhetoric Review** 13.2 (1995): 331–349.

Date: Sun, 1 Nov 1998 16:09:44 CST
From: sophist@UTARLG.UTA.EDU
To: Marshall Alcorn
Subject: vv>ma: Berlin discussion

Hi, Marshall. Some time ago, I wrote and told you about the Berlin Seminar. This week we will discuss your article. VVhich I just reread. (It's ever amazing how things are not seen first, second, etc. times around, until something clicks, and then there is the not-wanting-to-have-seen the thing/s. As if they are seen!)

I am writing for two reasons:

1. to ask if you would like to respond to grad student questions about your article. (they are good students; the seminar is going well. moreover, there are former grad students of Jim's on the list, who might like to ask questions or make comments.)

2. to ask if you would be interested in letting me publish the original-but-changed conclusion (p. 343) to the _RR_ article. I would like to publish it at the Berlin site, as "alternative 'original' ending," with the purpose of inviting others, like Berlin and unlike Berlin, to write still other alternative endings, perhaps picking up where Berlin and you (far) Left off. But of course I would like to publish it in the print version of *PRE/TEXT* also. As a means of letting print readers know about this continuing project that you helped start. I would create the mechanisms by way of Hyper News at the Berlin site for anyone to add on the WWW their alternative endings cum new beginnings. If you go to the Berlin Web site you will see what Hyper News looks like, if you do not already know. I would have to start a new HN site for just this collection of forthcoming alternative endings.

* * *

Date: Mon, 02 Nov 1998 16:47:21 -0500 (EST)

From: Marshall Alcorn
To: Victor Vitanza
Subject: Berlin (fwd)

Victor,

I have not compared this carefully with the original, but I know that this is what I cut when I decided to shorten and delete the ending that most of my readers found highly unclear. It probably is. In any event it will be interesting to see where exactly the problems are.
Thanks again, Marshall

When the conflicted codes of human subjectivity are brought into consciousness they are often not abandoned (as Berlin's argument implies), but instead re-affirmed even more insistently in the libidinal patterns of denial and repression that have defined them. All too often ideological conflicts are not abandoned because subjects have libidinal attachments to conflict. The symptoms of conflict as Lacan insists, are not something subjectivity can easily give up; the symptoms of conflict are not an accidental characteristics of subjectivity, they are subjectivity. This is true because subjectivity is a discourse (dis)organization that becomes (dis)organized as an effect of conflict. The understanding and recovery of unconscious conflict is not a self-indulgent project for personal fulfillment; it is a vital but difficult political goal. Mark Bracher in Lacan, Discourse, and Social Change asserts: "I would go so far as to say that without reducing the unconscious conflict—whether by individual psychoanalysis, by cultural criticism, or by various other means—the chances of reducing injustice and intolerance are virtually nonexistent" (192). Reducing unconscious conflict, Lacanian theory shows, is not a simple matter accomplished efficiently and effectively by rational and informative speech. Saying to a person "Look at these conflicting codes; you have unconscious conflict here," does not make the person recognize and resolve such conflict. This process of recognition (the central task of psychoanalysis but certainly not the exclusive domain of psychoanalysis) is made difficult because it is charged with all the processes of erotics, aggression, displacement and defense (those other meanings haunting Berlin's term "penetration") that subjects exhibit in maintaining their identities.

Often, for example, ideologies expressing prejudice are not simply conflicted discourse present in the structure of a subject. They are key defensive structures that help keep a vulnerable and conflicted system of subjectivity operating. They are like the walls or the moat that surrounds a fortress: the first line of defense, the point at which all battles are fought, the points of inspection past which nothing enters or exits the fortress. Prejudice defends the life of the subject, not the life of the biological individual, but the life of the ideological subject.

Just as patients in analysis often get worse before they get better, attacks upon prejudice in the classroom can generate increased hostility, irrationality, and paranoia, can in fact strengthen the defenses that preserve prejudice. Richard Boothby describes the "traumatized ego" that "draws back, as it were, to its last lines of defense and sandbags itself in a position that may be stable but only at the price of being highly constricted and ossified" (92). My point is not at all that we can do nothing about prejudice and the ossified ego. It is that it is our job to do something about it. But in order to do something about it, we must better understand how to talk to it and how to talk about it.

A psychoanalytic understanding of resistance enables us to formulate new strategies for dismantling prejudice. A major point here is that one does not overcome resistance by stating, explaining, restating, or insisting upon an apparently simple "truth" that resistance fortifies itself against. To overcome resistance, one does not focus upon the truth that needs to be learned, one instead focuses upon the nature and pattern of the discourse expressed in the resistance. The presence of resistance requires first, that teaching be a dialogue that generates trust, and second, that the teacher act as an ally of forces that a student wants to discover within herself— not as an embodiment of those forces in murderous opposition. Truth and rationality emerge in this scenario not as claims advocated by figures of authority, but as experiences of meaning discovered when all the internal repressed voices engaged in an important issue or event are fully heard. If, for the student, what is repressed is what is feared, then confronting the repressed is not facilitated by a purely rational discourse that further alienates the student from her persona life. Rational discourse becomes simply the terrain for verbal warfare.

Defending their prejudices, students are often moved to express various irrational defenses—denial, displacement, splitting, projection, or even physical violence—that serve to silence or dismiss voices of opposition. Teachers should learn to recognize and respond to these irrational defenses when they see them. These defensive responses, much more so than the beliefs they protect, can often be socialized into recognition and critical analysis. When we manage to do this—when we make repression an undesirable form of social behavior, when we unmask it as a weakness and not a strength. We can better pursue the goals of democracy, freedom and social-justice when we conceptualize a more complicated and realistic model of human subjectivity. We must more fully appreciate the character of resistance and make better use of Robert Con Davis' claim that "the resistance to learning. . .is learning itself" (626). It is pointless to continue to contrast the postmodern subject from the liberal human subject in terms of rationality or freedom. Rationality is not the goal of education, but when it understands the irrational networks of human identity, it is an important tool. When deftly employed it can an idealized middle term, even a transitional identity ("I will be rational, even though I don't like it.") that can allow students to move from one libidinally attached set of signifiers to another. Rather than abandon rationality, let us seek to understand how to use it. Rationality can be a libidinal tool effective in the push of libidinal language. It can be effective describing and even "penetrating" the irrational libidinal attachments that comprise ideological codes. Let me be more emphatic: rationality and literacy—the goals of educational practice—are not simple processes of moving knowledge from one person to another; they are complex processes deeply involved with gaining mastery over instinctive and irrational libidinal attachments.

Lacan argues that the "reality principle" that comes to define "realistic" adult thinking is itself always influenced by the libidinal operations of the "pleasure principle": "All thought by its very nature occurs according to unconscious means. It is doubtless not controlled by the pleasure principle, but it occurs in a space that as an unconscious space is to be considered as subject to the pleasure principle" (32). Rational thought then, for Lacan, is always a struggle to overcome or at least make intelligent use of the libidinal investments and unconscious patterns of perception and identification that always ground any real subjectivity or perception. Postmodernist theory generally ignores the libidinal complexity of speech and the libidinal organization of the human subject. Postmodernist theory generally describes the subject as a more or less simple collection of equally weighted discourse samples. Discourse surrounds and fills in and animates the subject. Considered in these terms, one is led to believe that one can change the subject simply by speaking more discourse. Let us be more rational. Let us seek to more fully understand the "penetrating" power of libidinal language and the defensive nature of libidinal attachments.

Subjectivity, Freud argues, is strongly coded by libidinal and imagistic attachments that develop through early experience. The child is first thrown into the world, not with language, but with a body. The child's earliest perceptions of the world are libidinal; they begin with bodily sensations of pleasure and pain, anticipation and avoidance. This organization of pleasure and pain becomes a preverbal and libidinal "language" that structures experience as bodily experience, and, in so doing, structures subjectivity itself. Joseph Smith points out that "Freud took preconscious organization as that which was accomplished preverbally. [I]t is this preverbal accomplishment that allows for speech" (24). This libidinal organization of experience encompasses Lacan's notion of the Imaginary and Freud's description of the ego as "the organized portion of the id." These libidinal organizations (influenced but not determined by ideological behavior) insure that the human subject is not a simple container of discourse; it is already from the beginning a particular libidinal organization of experience that structures in advance the meaning and experience of learned language. This preconscious organization of speech constructs subjectivity as an entity that is particularly conflicted in its organization of preverbal ideological experience and particularly repressed in its conflicts. This means that language is not present in the subject all in one neat, equal, and homogenous reservoir of cultural signifiers. Instead, subjects are constructed in terms of different and differently organized layers of differently weighted discourse.

Subjects contain a great deal of discourse, but some modes of discourse, because they are libidinally invested, repeatedly and predictably function to constitute the subject's sense of identity. Other instances of discourse, though contained by the subject, are not libidinally invested; this language may be "in" the subject but it simply lies dormant, having no effect whatever on subject functions. Consider an analogy to the computer. The language contained by the operating system of a computer is crucial in determining how the computer behaves. The language contained within the database of a computer, on the other hand, generally has no effect on how the computer behaves. Information contained within these two different levels of computer organization function very differently and may operate almost autonomously from each other. One instance of contained language operates the computer, the other instance is operated by the computer as the higher-level operating language directs it. If one were to enter the command "Stop" into a database, the computer could display this command, but this command would have no effect on the computer. It would continue to run. If one were to enter this command into the operating system, the computer would cease to operate. What matters in the discourse that subjects receive is not what is in the discourse, but where the discourse takes up residence in the organization of the subject. English teachers can teach a student to remember the ideas of Terry Eagleton, but the student may simply use these ideas as arguments to illustrate the failure of progressive education.

Humans, like computers, are organized by language, and like computers, process language according to different principles of operation that have been determined by their "basic" inner components. Human subjects, like computers, constantly interact with and employ the language of the external world. Human subjects, like computers, are very much an effect of discourse. But this description "effect of discourse" conceals the complex mechanisms that make both humans and computers something other than simple reflectors of external discourse.

Consider again the case of the British miner. The miner is, as we say, a construction of ideological codes. These ideological codes, however, are held in place by an organized and heterogenous collection of libidinal attachments tied both to language and to real people who represent linguistic abstractions. The miner is, for example, a son attached to a father, a son attached to a mother, to sisters, and brothers. Let us continue. He is attached to his friends, to pubs, darts, and beer, and we could go on and on. These living libidinal attachments, more so than abstract political ideas, are the building blocks of the miner's subjectivity.

If we imagine that the miner becomes a soldier not to defend the British system but to repeat his libidinal attachments we can begin to unravel some of the intersections of ideology and libidinal attachment. Masculinity, for example, is not a belief in the rational sense of the term; it is a lived, embodied relationship to a multitude of experiences. The soldier, defining himself through his work as a man, is attached in different intensities to a multitude of experiences that in the totality of their consciously and unconsciously lived experience (not in abstract thoughts) define what it means to be a man. Being a soldier reflects as a plenitude of very particular attachments many conscious and many unconscious. The miner has codes (or libidinal networks) of family attachments. (He wants to see himself as acting like other men in his family.) He has codes of regional attachment (He joins, for example, the Coldstream guards.) He expresses codes of adventure. (He wants to seek out exotic experiences that test his character and strength.) He expresses codes that define his bodily self-image. (He wants to see himself as strong, tall, and formidable.) He expresses codes of male bonding. (He wants to be recognized as part of a group of powerful males.) And he may express codes of rebellion. (He joins a combat unit that allows him to vent the anger and rage he feels toward the world.) If we think of the solider as a simple collection of abstractly defined ideological codes, we risk dismissing these libidinal codes and many others—others working in even more particular and more emphatically libidinal terms signified most intensely by particular personal memories and images—that construct the subject.

Freud argues that our libidinal attachments and detachments are not something that we can control through rational and abstract thought. In "Mourning and Melancholia" Freud points out that while we may know that a person we love is dead, we cannot simply abandon our libidinal attachments. We may logically "know" that who we love exists no more, and we may recognize that we must abandon our attachments. But contrary to our conscious decisions, our libidinal attachments persist in terms of memory, image, and emotion. The work of giving up attachments is not a simple rational decision, but a form of mourning. It is a complicated labor we perform upon the many and varied imagery of that which is lost. The work of mourning is always initially rejected, but later deeply absorbing and painful. This work is difficult, Freud says, because we must painfully withdraw our attachments from each and every memory image that still unconsciously maintains and insists upon maintaining our libidinal attachments. The person is mourning is like a youth who has lost his lover yet remains "attached" to her; he sees and feels her deeply haunting image everywhere he goes. Political attachments are not often as strong as attachments to parents and lovers. Nonetheless political identities reflect libidinal attachments. To understand ideology and its role in defining subjectivity we must better understand the nature of libidinal attachment. Often, for example, it can be counter-productive to seek to change political identity by simply talking more clearly about politics. For many subjects, a discussion of politics, in the common sense of the word, can be largely diversionary from the complex and adventitious patterns of discourse interaction that need to occur in order for the subject to divest itself of that knotted complex of conflicted libidinal organizations that in each concrete case define the subject and the political attachments of the community. Libidinal attachment is part of the condition of being human. Students come to our classes thoroughly knitted together by the libidinal forces of family relations, politics, and personal encounters with significant others. Rationality is not the condition of being human; it is an idealization (with different libidinal intensities for different subjects) made about linguistic activity that insists that under certain linguistic conditions subjects can be and should be "pushed" to recognize systematic relationships in language. Often these systematic relationships are conditions of attachment that cause suffering—both for ourselves and others. This system of relationships can be avoided, if we desire it, by changes we can make in those signifiers we choose for our attachments if we can be "pushed" or "moved" to be rational about such things.

If we cannot be rational, intelligent, and libidinally penetrating about what makes us suffer and how we can cure it, we can produce neither politics nor analysis; we will merely repeat the discourse of powerful ideologies without any hope of change. Our libidinal experience of suffering, our cognitive recognition of suffering and our rational plans to avoid it are at the center of our need for politics, and our need as well for self-consciously libidinal and libidinally rational expression.

Works Cited

Althusser, Louis "Ideology and Ideological State Apparatuses," in *Lenin and Philosophy and Other Essays by Louis Althusser.* Monthly Review Press, New York, 1971.

Berlin, James, "Poststructuralism, Cultural Studies, and the Composition Classroom: Postmodern Theory in Practice." *Rhetoric Review* 2 (Fall 1992): 16–33.

Boothby, Richard. *Death and Desire: Psychoanalytic Theory in Lacan's Return to Freud.* Routledge, New York, 1991.

Bracher, Mark. *Lacan, Discourse, and Social Change: A Psychoanalytic Cultural Criticism.* Ithaca: Cornell University Press, 1993.

Con Davis, Robert. "Freud's Resistance to Reading and Teaching." *College English* 49 (October 1987): 621–27.

Dews, Peter. *Logics of Disintegration.* London: 1987.

Eagleton, Terry. *An Introduction to Ideology.* London: Verso, 1991.

Freud, Sigmund. "Mourning and Melancholia." 1917. In *The Standard Edition of Complete Psycholobial Works of Sigmund Freud.* 24 vols. James Strachey ed. and trans. London: Hogarth Press, 1953–74, vol. 14: 237–260.

—. "Inhibitions, Symptoms and Anxiety." 1926. In *The Standard Edition*, vol 20: 77–179.

Lacan, Jacques. *Book VII. The Ethics of Psychoanalysis, 1959–1960, in The Seminar of Jacques Lacan.* Jacques-Alain Miller, ed., Sylvana Tomaselli trans. New York: W.W.Norton & Co., 1988.

Macdonell, Diane. *Theories of Discourse.* Oxford: Basil Blackwell, 1986.

Mogenson, Greg. "The Psychotherapy of the Dead: Loss and Character Structure in Freud's Metapsychology." *American Imago*, 45 (Fall 1988): 251–69.

Orwell, George. *Homage to Catalonia.* San Diego: Harcourt Brace, 1980.
Pecheux, Michel. *Language, Semantics and Ideology: Stating the Obvious,* trans. Harbans Nagpal. London: Macmillan Press, 1982.
Smith, Joseph H. *Arguing with Lacan: Ego Psychology and Language.* New Haven: Yale University Press, 1991.
Smith, Paul. *Discerning the Subject.* Minneapolis: University of Minnesota Press, 1988.
Wolfenstein, Eugene Victor, *Psychoanalytic Marxism.* New York: Guilford Press, 1993.
Žižek, Slavoj. *The Sublime Object of Ideology.* New York: Routledge, 1992.

The Wasteland Grows

This article—never published but disseminated as a plenary address to the Research Network Forum—supplements and complements the "Response" by Vitanza in **JAC** (1999) to Julie Drew's "(Teaching) Writing: Composition, Cultural Studies, Production," in **JAC** 19.3 (1999). 411–29. Make of it what you will. Among other things, Drew states: "Victor Vitanza dismissed what he calls 'cultural studies' as leading to 'cynicism and fascism,' and to viewing students as both 'objects' and 'products' in his rather polemical address. . . ." (411).

Victor J. Vitanza, "The Wasteland Grows," Research Network Forum, College Composition and Communication Conference, Chicago, April, 1998.

> *The wasteland grows: woe to him who hides wastelands within.*
> *–Nietzsche*

I've been asked to talk about rhetorical theory and focus my discussion in terms of needed research. I am going to limit my talk. I will focus specifically on what I consider to be an important problem—if not, the problem—in rhetoric and composition theory and pedagogy. I am simply going to toss the problem out for your consideration.

I want to talk about cultural studies or cultural critique or cultural criticism or whatever you wish to call it. I am aware that each of these is theoretically different—and according to a variety of schools—but I purposefully conflate them, for they are the same essentially in their reliance on bringing Reason to bear on ethical-political problems. On Social Change. I want to raise a question about the value of such areas of 'thought-thinking-thought' that would teach students to identify the contradictions in the social fabric and to set about correcting those contradictions. Specifically, as a long-standing member of the Research Forum, I want to question, or have you question, in the name of 'making knowledge' (doing research), whether or not teaching students cultural studies and other similar studies makes them seek for a better world that is obtainable. I want to suggest to you, on the contrary, that cultural studies may lead only to cynicism. May be for the most part producing several generations of students who will have become cynics—more cynical than cynical. Hyper-cynical! Trans-cynical! If this suggestion of a claim does not piss off some people in the epistemic court, then I don't know what will!

But let me say that I sincerely do not want to infuriate my colleagues in rhetoric or composition or more specifically in the social-epistemic schools, mainly because I want them to listen, really listen, for their own goods, to what I am suggesting. I say "for their own good[s]" with a pun on the word goods. Yes, I refer to my colleagues' commodities, not just to the economics of their thinking about liberating students in writing classrooms so as to bring about social change, but to the new generations of cynics that they may very well be producing. This is my concern: not the Mods, not the Post mods, but the commodities. The Objects being produced who believe. I doubt it anymore that subjects are taught to know or to believe; I am beginning to think, as Marx suggests that Objects know and believe. And that perhaps they will always remain Objects. And I am beginning to believe that they will have their revenge. (Yes, I am alluding to Jean Baudrillard thoughts on this point.)

Hear me carefully: I am not saying that such student-objects are, in fact, being produced on a small scale or large one. It is only my belief, my hunch that they are. I am saying that, instead, it should be part of the very research and pedagogical protocols of theoreticians and teachers of cultural studies, to be concerned ethically and politically with their productions. They should be concerned in their research as to whether or not their product is a safe product. By safe, I mean one that, in fact, moves itself and us toward a better life! I will pick up this issue again later, but for now. . . . Let me establish a brief historical context and then I want to rebegin with, I hope, a

In speaking about cultural studies or critique or whatever, I could go back to Plato or Aristotle or move up to Kant (especially his "What is the Enlightenment?" essay) or to Foucault (with his counter-Kantian Enlightenment essay), or I could start from the experiences of those of us who grew up academically and socially in the late 60s and early 70s, but I want, instead, to go back to Paul Ricoeur, who coins the term "the hermeneutics of suspicion" (Freud 32). I think that Ricoeur best describes—sentimentally—modernist notions of liberation from false consciousness. In speaking of interpretation as an ex(er)cise of suspicion, Ricoeur distinguishes between "the school of reminiscence" ("recollection of meaning") and "the school of suspicion" ("reduction of the illusions and lies of consciousness") (32). Ricoeur focuses on Marx, Nietzsche, and Freud, who as hermeneuts have in common "the decision to look upon the whole of consciousness primarily as 'false' consciousness" (33). In this light Ricoeur sees the three thinkers moving beyond Descartes and his doubt, by placing the consciousness of the Cartesian thinker itself under suspicion. Then, Ricoeur says that the three hermeneuts—Marx and others—are no mere "masters of skepticism" because each "clear[s] the horizon for a more authentic word, for a new reign of Truth, not only by means of 'destructive' critique, but by the invention of an art of interpreting" (35).

Ricoeur depicts Marx and then Nietzsche and Freud in a narrative of Enlightenment. Hence, they are liberators. They become aware, given the archaeological model, that there is a depth at which the truth resides and hides. The surface is superficial in the most negative sense of the word superficial; the depth holds the condition for the possibilities of truth. Social Justice. It is from this realization of the depth model that the three hermeneuts of suspicion begin to write and speak of the effect of ideology. As Marx says best about ideology in Capital I, "they [the masses] do this [bring their products and value together] without being aware of it" (166–67). The basic assumption (that Marx and many of us make with this statement) is that if the masses knew they did or are doing it, they would stop it!

My sense, however, for many who see and strip away false consciousness, there is no liberation or cure, but only an ever-growing cynicism, an ever-growing wasteland within them, or what Peter Sloterdijk calls in *The Critique of Cynical Reason* an "enlightened false consciousness" (*Critique* 5). Growing within them. Sloterdijk writes:

> Cynicism is enlightened false consciousness. It is that modernized, unhappy consciousness, on which enlightenment has labored both successfully and in vain. It has learned its lessons in enlightenment, but it has not, and probably was not able to, put them into practice. Well-off and miserable at the same time, this consciousness no longer feels affected by any critique of ideology; its falseness is already reflexively buffered. (5)

This view is echoed and made even more problematic by many others who critique critique. For example, in The Sublime Object of Ideology, Slavoj Žižek, writes:

> we can account for the formula of cynical reason proposed by Sloterdijk: "they know very well what they are doing, but still, they are doing it." If the illusion were on the side of knowledge, then the cynical position would really be a post-ideological position, simply a position without illusions: "they know what they are doing, and they are doing it." But if the place of the illusion is in the reality of doing itself, then this formula can be read in quite another way: "they know that, in their activity, they are following an illusion, but still, they are doing it." For example, they know that their idea of Freedom is masking a particular form of exploitation, but they still continue to follow this idea of Freedom. (33)

There are many other combinations and permutations based on this formula: 'they do it, but don't know they do it.' Or, 'they do it and know that they do it.' These combinations and permutations all come down to one strong notion: A de-territorialization followed by a reterritorialization, in the scene(s) of cultural critique, does not bring the expected liberation. Stripping away false consciousness may lead but to enlightened false consciousness. Reason/rationality, when used to expose what it foresees as superstition, magic, etc., is a banal strategy. (By 'banal strategy' I mean the militaristic use of Reason to win out over what is called superstition, magic, etc.) The promise of Reason, the Enlightenment, the promise of Liberation, has brought fascism, as Sloterdijk argues extensively in his near 600-page book. Enlightenment (rationality), cynicism, and fascism are often co-conspirators. But we have, nonetheless, a way of co-deflecting-and-forgetting all these connections and histories. Given the limits of time, I cannot rehearse Sloterdijk's extensive argument here; a careful reading and studying of the book on your parts are necessary. Chapter 4—"After the Unmaskings: Cynical Twilight. Sketches for the Self-repudiation of the Ethos of Enlightenment"—is a devastating critique, in which Sloterdijk uses reason contra reason on his way to unfolding "The Weimar Symptom: Models of Consciousness in German Modernity."

And yet—look into your minds!—my telling you of Sloterdijk's position can bring but forgetfulness itself. Bring but silence. Bring but rolling eyes to members of the audience. Right? I can overhear someone thinking: "Well, Really, Really, Victor, How could anyone who is concerned with developing a discipline or any disciplinary thinking be concerned with the idea of forsaking Reason/rationality!! And what's this stuff about Enlightenment thinking leading to fascism?!"

What to do? With this problem of Thinking—What is called Thinking?—which precedes the problem of Enlightenment Thinking. (Yes, I know, I am remaining somewhat obscure with this last point; for I do not want you to hear with full volume and with full sense what I would—if all else fails—have you, my colleagues, do in replacing y/our banal strategies.)

But lest I give too much to think about, this is what I would openly suggest that cultural studies researchers—that is, you who are theorists and practitioners and others—DO: Not only teach the basic principles of critiquing the culture at all levels (I am not calling for the abolition of cultural studies!) but also and more so be vigilant now about the effects such teaching have on your students and consequently on the rest of us. On the Social fabric. (Part of our grossest national product is cynicism!) But you will have to be more than just vigilant, right? You who are researchers. What I would have you do is engage in a series of longitudinal studies, following, tracking your students, to see what they will have learned in terms of your teaching them cultural studies. The primary question in such a study would have to be, Do the students ever stop thinking and practicing racism, sexism, classism, age-ism, do they ever stop thinking and practicing their homophobia and self-hatred, etc., or do they, in taking on an understanding of false consciousness in your "class"rooms, only become more cynical in their acts of violence against other human beings and themselves? In other words, Do they know such thinking and acting are wrong but do it anyway?

Let me close on a pleasant yet ever-haunting memory in the form of an anecdote that would be an antidote: I will never forget the honesty—the brute and raw honesty—of Jim Berlin, when, at the Marxist Literary Group at CMU, he delivered a paper questioning his success as a teacher of social liberation. He reported on a student who fully understood how he was being manipulated by the media machine, understood how he had become an object in the media-scape, but nonetheless continued cynically to purchase the products that were the object of his media-driven desire. Yes, the student was but an object purchasing objects! After all, when everything was said and undone, the student desired something to believe in and to believe for him!

Jim cited this example so as to turn it into a question for the audience; namely, How might we take this and other similar students to the other side of what we might deem social liberation? The audience that Jim addressed that evening at the MLG, however, was silent in response to his question! I was on the same panel with Jim. Though we had not planned antithetical positions, I attempted to break the silence by raising the counter-question of Whether or not we who taught cultural studies, etc., were producing a generation of cynics, as I have once again attempted to ask here today. Yet there was only more silence. There before us: Gawking Silence!! Plenty people in the audience had read Marx and Marxists and Post Marxists and had read Sloterdijk! (In fact, if I were to list some of their names here, you would surely agree that it was in part a list of 'Whose Who' in cultural studies, in cultural theory, in cultural critique.) There was, however, but silence. And to this day for the most part there remains only silence. We can no longer be complicit with this y/our silence.

Therefore, I would humbly call for major research efforts to determine the success or failure—and longitudinally—of whether cultural studies theorists and pedagogues are socially liberating students or producing but cynics or worse producing liberated students who are but incipient cynics. Producing but wastelands within them and their own children and students. And on and on geometrically. Virulently. Thank you.

Works Cited

Foucault, Michel. "What Is Enlightenment?" in *Foucault Reader*. Ed. Paul Rabinow. New York: Pantheon, 1984. 32–50.

Kant, Immanuel. "What Is Enlightenment?" in *Philosophical Writings*. Ed. Ernst Behler. New York: Continuum, 1986.

Marx, Karl. *Capital*. Vol. 1. NY: Vintage, 1977.

Ricoeur, Paul. *Freud and Philosophy*. Trans. Denis Savage. New Haven: Yale UP, 1978.

Sloterdijk, Peter. *The Critique of Cynical Reason*. Trans. Michael Eldred. Minneapolis: U of Minnesota P, 1987.

Žižek, Slajov. *The Sublime Object of Ideology*. New York: Verso, 1989.

But there are more for the seminar →

Major Texts

Berlin, James A. "Composition Studies and Cultural Studies: Collapsing Boundaries." **Into the Field: Sites of Composition Studies**. Ed. Anne Ruggles Gere. New York: MLA,1993. 99–116.

—. "Composition and Cultural Studies." **Composition and Resistance**. Eds. Hurlbert, C. Mark and Michael Blitz. Portsmouth: NH: Boynton/Cook, 1991.

—. "Contemporary Composition: The Major Pedagogical Theories." **College English** 44 (1982): 765–77.

—-. "Cultural Studies." **Encyclopedia of Rhetoric and Composition**. Ed. Theresa Enos. New York: Garland, 1996. 154–56.

—. "Freirean Pedagogy in the U.S.: A Response." **Journal of Advanced Composition** 12 (Fall 1992): 414–421.

—. "James Berlin Responds. 'Rhetoric and Ideology in the Writing Class.'" **College English** 51 (1989): 770–77.

—. "Postmodernism, Politics, and Histories of Rhetorics." **PRE/TEXT** 11.3–4 (1990): 169–187.

—. "Poststructuralism, Cultural Studies, and the Composition Classroom." **Rhetoric Review** 11 (Fall 1992): 16–33. Rpt. **Professing the New Rhetoric**. Ed. Theresa Enos and Stuart C. Brown. Englewood Cliffs, New Jersey: Prentice-Hall, 1994. 461–80.

—. "Revisionary History: The Dialectical Method." **PRE/TEXT** 8.1–2 (1987): 47–61.

—. "Revisionary Histories of Rhetoric: Politics, Power, and Plurality." **Writing Histories of Rhetoric**, ed. Victor J. Vitanza. Carbondale: Southern Illinois UP, 1994. 112–27.

—. "Rhetoric and Ideology in the Writing Class." **College English** 50 (1988): 477–494.

—. **Rhetorics, Poetics, and Cultures: Refiguring College English Studies**. Urbana: NCTE, 1996.

—. "Rhetoric and Poetics in the English Department: Our Nineteenth-Century Inheritance." **College English** 47 (1985): 531–33.

—. **Rhetoric and Reality: Writing Instruction in American Colleges. 1900–1985**. Carbondale: Southern Illinois UP, 1987.

—. "Richard Whately and Current-Traditional Rhetoric." **College English** 42 (September 1980): 10–17.

—. **Writing Instruction in Nineteenth-Century American Colleges**. Carbondale: Southern Illinois UP, 1984.

Berlin, James A., et al. Octalog. "The Politics of Historiography." **Rhetoric Review** 7 (1988): 5–49.

Berlin, James A., and Robert P. Inkster. "Current-Traditional Rhetoric: Paradigm and Practice." **Freshman English News** 8. 3 (Winter 1980): 1–4, 13–14.

Major Edited Works

Berlin, James A., and Michael Vivion, eds. **Cultural Studies in the English Classroom**. Portsmouth, NH: Boynton,/Cook, Heinman, 1992.

Berlin, James A., and John Trimbur, guest eds. Special Issue: "Marxism and Rhetoric." **PRE/TEXT** 13. 1–2. (1992).

Major Secondary Material (directed Berlin)

Anderson, Virginia. "Property Rights: Exclusion as Moral Action in 'The Battle of Texas.'" *College English*, 62.4 (2000): 445–72.

Alcorn, Marshall. "Changing the Subject of Postmodernist Theory: Discourse, Ideology, and Therapy in the Classroom." *Rhetoric Review* 13.2 (1995): 331–49.

Bizzell, Patricia. "Beyond anti-Foundationalism Rhetorical Authority: Problems Defining 'Cultural Literacy.'" *College English* 52.6 (1990): 661–75. (Critique of Berlin on pp. 670, 672–73.)

Brodkey, Linda. *Academic Writing as Social Practice*. Philadelphia: Temple UP, 1987.

Brodlkey, Linda. *Writing Permitted in Designated Areas*. Minneapolis: U of Minnesota P, 1996. (more of The Battle of Texas)

Connors, Robert J. Rev. of *Writing Instruction in Nineteenth-Century American Colleges*, James A. Berlin. *College Composition and Communications* 37 (1986): 247–49.

Crowley, Sharon. Rev of *Rhetoric and Reality: Writing Instruction in American Colleges: 1900–1985*, James A. Berlin. *College Composition and Communications* 39 (1986): 245–47.

Downing, David B., James J. Sosnoski, with Keith Dorwick, eds. Cultural Studies and Composition: Conversations in Honor of James Berlin. *Works and Days* 14.1–2 (1996).

Faigley, Lester. *Fragments of Rationality: Postmodernity and the Subject of Composition*. Pittsburgh: U of Pittsburgh P, 1992.

Findley, Barbara with Paul W.Rea. "Interview with Mazine Hairston. *Rhetoric Review*, Vol. 8, No. 2, Spring 1990

Flower, Linda. "Comments on James Berlin. 'Rhetoric and Ideology in the Writing Class.'" *College English* 51 (1989): 765–69.

"Future Perfect, Tense" (A collection of articles by Linda Brodkey, Patricia Harkin, Susan Miller, John Trimbur, and Victor J. Vitanza on *Rhetorics, Poetics, Cultures*). *Journal of Advanced Composition* 17.3 (1997): 489–505. (Jim Berlin's Last Work)

Schilb, John. "Comments on James Berlin. 'Rhetoric and Ideology in the Writing Class.'" *College English* 51 (1989): 769–70.

Scriben, Karen. "Comments on James Berlin. 'Rhetoric and Ideology in the Writing Class.'" *College English* 51 (1989): 764–65.

Vitanza, Victor J. "James A. Berlin." *Twentieth-Century Rhetorics and Rhetoricians: Critical Studies and Sources*. Ed. Michael G. Moran and Michelle Ballif. Westport, CT: Greenwood P, 2000. 32–43.

Major Secondary Material (used by Berlin)

Fogarty, Daniel. *Roots for a New Rhetoric*. New York: Teachers College P, 1959.

Freire, Paulo. *Pedagogy of the Oppressed*. New York: Continuum, 1970.

Kitzhaber, Albert R. "Rhetoric in American Colleges, 1850–1900." Diss. Washington U, 1953; in published form, *Rhetoric in American Colleges, 1850–1900*. Dallas, TX: Southern Methodist UP, 1990.

Ohmann, Richard. *English in America: A Radical View of the Profession*. New York: Oxford UP, 1976.

Shor, Ira. *Critical Teaching and Everyday Life*. Chicago: U of Chicago P, 1987.

Therborn, Goran. *The Ideology of Power and the Power of Ideology*. London: Verso, 1980.

Williams, Raymond. *Keywords: A Vocabulary of Culture and Society*. Revised Edition. New York: Oxford UP, 1977.

Major Sources

- Purdue Berlin archives // http://berlinproject.donaldunger.com/
- Dr. James Berlin: A Champion for Composition. ENGL 5360 Podcast Series Texas Tech University / Hosted by: Hugh Pressley // https://www.youtube.com/watch?v=tfIhLlSYqtg

About the Author

VICTOR J. VITANZA is a Professor Emeritus of English and Founding Director of the PhD transdisciplinary program in Rhetorics, Communication, and Information Design at Clemson University. Prior to joining the Clemson faculty, he was a Professor of English at the University of Texas at Arlington, where he developed and coordinated the Rhetoric emphasis for the PhD in Humanities and later co-wrote the PhD for English (Rhetoric and Literature tracks).

VV also served as Professor of Rhetoric and Philosophy, as well as the Jean-François Lyotard Professor, at the European Graduate School, Saas-Fee, Switzerland, in the Media and Communication program, from 2002 until 2018.

VV is the author of *Negation, Subjectivity, and the History of Rhetoric* (SUNY, 1997) and *Sexual Violence in Western Thinking and Writing: Chaste Rape* (Palgrave, 2011). Both are the first two volumes in his Trilogy. . . . He has edited and contributed to *PRE/TEXT: The First Decade* (U of Pittsburgh P, 1993) and *Writing Histories of Rhetoric* (SIUP, 1994, 2013), among many other books and journals. He founded *PRE/TEXT* in 1983 and has been its editor for thirty-seven years. His next book, *A Rethinking of Historiographies (of Rhetorics) as Atemporal, Anachronistic Post-Cinematic Practices*, will be published by Parlor Press in 2021.

Photograph of the author by Clemson Photo Services. Used by permission.

www.ingramcontent.com/pod-product-compliance
Lightning Source LLC
Chambersburg PA
CBHW060941170426
43195CB00026B/2996